The secretary of the Idaho Education Association has said — and I quote: "We cannot afford to reorganize our school curricula in the interests of the gifted if by so doing we dilute the opportunity of those not so endowed. We cannot establish minimum standards at any grade which, when rigorously applied will result in those failing to achieve them being 'spelled down' and 'out'." What we need, of course, is schools for training in different skills, and schools (we'd not need many) for those who seek education and have the capacity for it. Harvard's Talcott Parsons says, "Probably the best single index of the line between upper middle class and the rest of the middle class is the *expectation* that children will have a college education as a matter that is a status right." Lee J. Cronbach, a leading educational psychologist, asks, "Can we be sure that punctuality and self-control and effort are better values than casualness and self-expression and enjoyment of the moment?" Life-adjustment has become the cry in our schools, but as the California Citizens Advisory Committee has recently reported, after a long investigation of the schools, it is not education at all. It is not even training. As for the educational psychologists, they are little more than brash adolescents who are trying to interpret what they have no sense of.

I'm going to tell you what I think education is, not by defining it in a few words, but by talking about a few matters, such as evidence. But because this is a drearily heavy subject, and because Americans must have a light moment after a heavy moment, let us revert again to Schoenberner, the European intellectual. Quote: "The writer recalled how, after a performance of Medea, he had overheard the bitter complaint that there had not been the slightest comic relief, not a single occasion for a laugh. And he remembered the story of the farmer who, after a terrible hell-fire sermon, challenged the preacher's warning of eternal damnation with the words, 'The people won't stand for that.'"

Some of you may be old enough to remember the frenzied hullabaloo over the conviction in 1921 of Sacco and Vanzetti for murder. In its hysterias and frenzies it was far more extreme than the recent agitation over Chessman. I was at the time a young wild-eyed liberal; I thought the *New Republic* and the *Nation* told the truth and all the truth, and with thousands of people I detested the judge and the state of Massachusetts. Recently I have read Robert Montgomery's "The Murder and the Myth," and Judge Musmanno's "The Verdict." Both men are distinguished lawyers. Both examined all the known evidence. Montgomery has no doubt the men were guilty; Musmanno has no doubt they were innocent. I read all the evidence they presented and could reach no conclusion.

I have spent a good part of the past two years doing research for a book on the death of Meriwether Lewis. I have talked about the matter with various scholars and historians and haven't yet found one who does not think that Lewis killed himself. Not one of them has examined more than a part of the evidence that I have examined. Quite recently a distinguished historian has read my manuscript. Before reading it he had no doubt that Lewis killed himself. After reading it he wrote me that "You have convinced me that James Neelly was dishonest and that Mrs. Grinder was a real nut." He still thinks Lewis killed himself. With the possible exception of Lewis's servant the only witnesses the proponents of suicide have is a man this historian now thinks was dishonest, and a woman he thinks was a nut.

The capacity of the human mind to rationalize in favor of what the emotions want to believe is beyond all power of exaggeration. In most persons education makes little headway against it. There is a story that was told first of a French judge, that no doubt has since been applied to others. Observing at what promised to be a sensational and shocking trial that the courtroom was jammed with women he said, "I must ask all the decent women to withdraw." When not a single woman rose and left the court he said angrily, "Now that the decent women have left the officials will remove the others." Whether the women or the judge was the prejudiced party most persons would determine in favor of their prepossessions.

If I were again to teach, the course I'd prefer above all others would be one in the nature of evidence. What is the evidence? has long been my favorite question. I have found that few people seem to know what evidence is. Now if it is not one of the first functions of education — not training but education — to teach people how to evaluate evidence, it is not the kind of education I am talking about.

We all know that in the physical sciences, persons are soon discredited who reach conclusions on any ground but verifiable evidence.

155

We all know that in the social sciences it should be that way but is not. To be sure, it is much easier in the exact sciences to establish fact or probability; but that this is so in no way absolves us from trying to establish the facts and probabilities in all fields. We all know what fools Soviet leaders made of themselves when for political reasons they tried to alter or deny conclusions that had come from the world's laboratories. We know how childlike and unrealistic certain eminent scientists have been when, stepping out of their fields, they pronounced judgments not on facts but on emotions. And we know that when Soviet leaders exempt fields from intellectual inquiry it is only for reasons of political expediency, and not, as in the western world, because in so many ways leadership is still enslaved by primitive beliefs and explanations.

I think we must admit that we do not have much education in this country, if we mean not the mere acquisition of knowledge or the training in skills but the use of knowledge to develop the full man and promote intelligent living. That is the ideal, of course. Possibly mankind came closest to it in ancient Greece and in the Renaissance, when the development of the fully rounded man was declared to be the function of education. How can we have education in a democracy when the very materials and methods in our schools are in so many ways determined by those who are least qualified for the task?

Early this year I published a novel that has been called controversial. Anything is controversial that runs contrary to the traditions and conventions. It is said in this book that most children do not mature and become adults, as the children of all other animals do, because their growth is stunted by those revered values in a religious system which is essentially an idealization of the family relationship. The thing called togetherness has become a disease in this country — at the recent Republican convention we had the distressing spectacle of a Mr. Nixon accepting a nomination and thanking the multitude before him for the love presented (that was his word for it) to him, his wife, his children, his mother. Apparently his dog was not there.

A psychologist challenged me to give my criteria of adultness. I dashed off a few random thoughts about the hypothetical adult — that he surely understands and accepts Baur's words, "There can be no true objective criticism until a man stands more or less indifferent to the result." Of how many can you say that they accept the facts and the probabilities *in all fields?* Of how many can you say that they have a well-developed sense, untouched by emotion and self-interest, of the laws of evidence, and know that the laws are valid in all fields?

This hypothetical adult (I wrote the psychologist) has tried to look to the sources of *all* his beliefs. Of how many can you say that? He holds no opinions merely because they were taught him by parents and schools. He is willing to allow to his children the fullest possible development of their talents, uninfluenced by his own tastes and preferences. Of how many parents can you say that? He holds no beliefs under which there seems not to be substantial and demonstrable support. Of how many can you say that?

The adult assumes that understanding motivations is almost the first law of his nature, and self-discipline the second. We don't expect him to share mass enthusiasms, despairs, hysterias, or to participate with immature persons in idolatries, cults, fads; or to identify himself with groups, parties, sects, nationalisms, or races. He understands that exploitation is the first law of ape-nature, and that only occasionally does a human being emerge from the sub-human mass. He knows that all but adults are the victims of propaganda, lies and hysterias, and a multitude of appeals to a low order of self-interest. Detached but compassionate, he no longer has what Ellen Glasgow called the illusion of disillusionment, the trademark of the cleverer adolescent journals, like the *New Yorker.* He knows that the conflict of wills has its sources and motivations not in principles, but in aggressions born of hungers, vanities, distortions, and fears.

Who is most like him? Oh, maybe a few — there are some, including the author of *Ecclesiastes* — who are aware not only of the fantastic vanity of most persons, but of the fantastic inadequacy of even the ablest minds. You all know that millions of words have been written the past few years about the forthcoming exploration of the universe. In magazines have appeared letters (by college graduates, I assume) that have said that if Columbus could find a new hemisphere, there is nothing to stop us in disposing of our surplus population, if not our wheat, in other solar systems. Certain religious organizations have solemnly considered such a plan. This nonsense comes from more than failure in education; it comes from failure to impart even the fundamentals of knowledge.

I'll let Bertrand Russell speak from *The Impact of Science on Society*: "There is an incredible amount of empty space in the universe. The distance from the sun to the nearest star is about 4.2 light years. This is in spite of the fact that we live in an exceptionally crowded part of the universe, namely, the Milky Way, which is an assemblage of about 300,000 million stars. This assemblage is one of an immense number of similar assemblages; about 30 million of them are known. The average distance from one to the next is about two million light years."

As you know, a light-year is the distance light travels in a year, at 186,000 miles a second — or 24 times sixteen billion miles. It takes 4.2 light-years, or 1533 times 16 billion, for light to travel to the star out there nearest our own. That star is 2336 plus ten zeroes away. Call it 23 trillion miles. Then bear in mind that between any two of the 30 million known milky ways the average distance is not 23 trillion miles, but five hundred thousand times that.

Man will go to the moon but the moon is only a little over a second of light-speed away from us. He may go to Mars — that is only a few light-seconds away. He stands about as much chance to reach another solar system as a colony of ants stands to cross the ocean and drive the Communists out of Asia. The wonder to me is that people can spend sixteen years in our public schools and have no better than an utterly childish notion of the universe.

The fact is that education in our country is less, not more, than it used to be. If the steady debauchery of our school system is to be stopped and its quality improved, I should think that you librarians might take a powerful hand in the matter, for vested in you are fairly broad and discriminatory powers in the choice and promotion of books. Oh, I know that in many ways your hands are tied: I have studied the librarians in four university and several public libraries and they have all looked to me like harassed people, who would do better than they do if they were not up against the monolithic ignorance and prejudice of school boards and alumni. I now and then recall with a chuckle the time at the University of Utah when the librarian was driven out of her wits by the famous "Hatrack" article in the *American Mercury* — the one about the prostitute who took her Catholic patrons into the Protestant cemetery, and her Protestants into the Catholic. What a remarkably educated person she must have been!

Because of this barbarous conflict with the gangsters in the Kremlin you librarians must find your task more difficult than it used to be. Various forces, hiding behind righteousness and patriotism, have organized drives against your citadels, sometimes with amusing and sometimes with serious results. The suppressions have gone so far into bigotry and lunacy that broadcasting companies, it is said, will no longer allow on their programs such words as nigger or darkey. The Stephen Foster songs seem to be only one remove from outright treason. Even *Huckleberry Finn* is being thrown out, though the character who elicits the most sympathy in that book is a darkey.

In a nation of educated adults such idiocies could not prevail, much less become popular. According to a recent book, one of these NAACP Hoffas went to a certain librarian and demanded that a certain book be withdrawn. The librarian protested. She tried to get the fellow to talk sense. She said, "Look, there are hundreds of books published that contain objectionable words — why yes, even the Bible. Or Shakespeare. The word bastard must occur twenty times in his plays. Are you going to throw Shakespeare out?"

The custodian of public morals looked at her and scratched his woolly head. Like Miniver Cheevey he thought and thought about it. Then he said, "Lady, I just wouldn't know about that. But mebbe them bastards ain't as well organized as us niggers is."

Well, ladies and gentlemen, there will be a lot of time for improvement after you and I are dead. There may be whole light-years of time. What did Omar say? — When you and I behind the veil are past, oh, but the long long while the world will last! And a better world, no doubt, it will be. Some of us, too impatient perhaps, want a better world now.

My Bible Heritage

Budd Schulberg published a novel about a Hollywood heel called *What Makes Sammy Run?* Thomas Wolfe published various novels, all about himself, in an effort to explain what made Wolfe run. Many years ago I published four novels, widely assumed to have been auto-biographical, in which I sought to explain what made the man run. None of us was successful for the reason that the man is not in the child. He is in all centuries of human history.

After this conviction had matured in my mind I hung above my desk Stekel's famous words, "When mankind desires to create something big it must reach down deep into the reservoir of its past," and set before myself a program of quite prodigious reading, and eleven historical novels, from our earliest beginnings to the present time. My first task was to learn, if I could, which ideas, symbols and peoples had most to do with shaping us today in the Western world, and which periods or conflicts were the most crucial. As the past began to come into perspective, after many years of intensive reading, it

---

* First published in *The American Zionist*, November 5, 1953.

seemed to me that the ancient Hebrew people would have to be given at least three of the eleven novels. Some readers have challenged me on that; they have felt that not more than one book in eleven, covering so many tens of thousands of years, should be given to any one people. They may be right and I may be wrong. It may be that because the Bible had upon me such a profound and lasting influence it was my tendency to exaggerate its influence on the Western world.

I was an abnormally terrified, serious, and studious child. Living far from human settlements and not entering school until I was about twelve, I learned to read at a very early age, and read everything that our impoverished home afforded, including the Bible. I read that book at least two or three times before I reached adolescence. Looking back, I'd say that it frightened more than it edified me, abashed more than it filled. A child can hardly be expected to grasp its parables, and above all it is a book of parables. In our copy were illustrations — of Samson tearing down the pillars, of David slaying the giant, of Noah offering thanksgiving; and though the physical feats caught my fancy, the deepest impression on me was made by the faces of the great prophets, admonishing, exhorting, or denouncing their people. They were fearful faces to look at (and are in many of the celebrated paintings of them), the faces of very strong and very angry men, invoking the wrath of God upon the wickedness of his children.

After reading in the book a day or two, I would suffer nightmares. If ever a child thought he was doomed, that child was I, listening while lying awake at night to the awful fury of a great river, hurling its forces against the stone walls of its deep gorge, and seeing almost as plain as if he stood before me the angry face of a prophet, as with clenched hands and enraged eyes he denounced the evils among his people.

I never lost my interest in the Bible; no man could into whom it has gone as deep as it went into me. I read it through carefully in my middle twenties, when I was laid up because I had almost cut a foot off. Even after so many years the childhood terrors returned. A little later I began to read about it, in the great scholars, and with interruptions have pursued that study ever since, branching out after a while into the fields of learning most closely allied to it. Still later,

I began to read the Jewish scholars, and have read more than fifty of the ablest.

Jewish scholars have again and again pointed out that Christian scholars, or, better, non-Jewish, since not all of them are Christians, in the field of Higher Criticism, would do well to read a little more in ancient Jewish writings, if they would more fully understand these matters, and the New Testament particularly. Herford and Moore and some others have read widely in Jewish scholarship and in the old Hebrew texts. But many Biblical scholars, alas, have not.

When this became plain to me, I began to read in those ancient writings. The sum of them is, of course, simply immense, and no man could hope to have the time to read all of it. But it is necessary, I am sure, to read a part of it if one would understand the people who produced it. And to read not only the more familiar parts of the Talmud and the well-known Pirke Aboth from the Mishnah and in the homiletical Midrash, but to read the Jewish scholars as well, such as Montefiore, Loewe, Margolis, Baron, Finkelstein, Ginzberg, Kohler, Schechter, and others. It is a peculiar kind of presumption that expects to understand the New Testament when the person is ignorant of such great works as Montefiore's *Rabbinic Literature and Gospel Teaching* and such interpretations of Judaism as those by Schechter and Abrahams.

The more one reads in these fields the more one becomes aware of the deep and abiding moral earnestness of the Hebrew people, or at least of their religious leaders, not alone in the past twenty centuries, not only in such as Maimonides, Akiba, Hillel, but almost as far back as the records go. For one who does not believe in "revelation," this moral earnestness, without parallel and apparently without precedent, is one of the riddles of history. I know of no one who has tried to explain it on a rational basis. But whatever its source, it is precisely our strength which totalitarian ideologies would now corrupt and destroy. Early Christianity, to be sure, drew from all sources in the Roman world, notably from the Gnostics and Stoics, from Plato and Buddha, but chiefly from Judaism; for no matter how far the leaders tried to move away from the Jews — and they strove desperately and long — Judaism remained at the heart of their faith. As Max Margolis says, in outward appearance the Orient was subjected by the Occident, "but inwardly the West really succumbed to the East."

On how completely it succumbed authorities differ. For Dean Inge, "These two streams, the Semitic and the European, the Jewish and the Greek, still mingle their waters in the turbid flood which constitutes the institutional religion of civilized humanity; but to this day the waters flow side by side in the same bed, perfectly recognizable, so alien are the two types to each other." Prof. Joseph Klausner, a Jew, has put it this way: "Judaism and Christianity are not only two different religions, but they are also *two different world views* [his italics]. Judaism will never allow itself to reach even in theory the ethical extremeness characteristic of Christianity; this extremeness has no place in the world of reality." No doubt there is truth in both statements, and for reasons that it would be interesting to explore. How difficult, then, for any person brought up in the Christian traditions to say precisely in what ways the Bible has influenced him!

Oesterley and Robinson, two Higher Critics, may cast a little light on this difficult matter when they say that there "is a fundamental difference in outlook between the Semitic and the Indo-European mind . . . the latter has invariably tended to become pantheistic. . . . The Semitic mind laid intense stress on personality." It is that intense stress on personality, on the dignity of the individual before God, on free will and moral choice, that has modified the fundamental difference in outlook, for all these are now characteristic of Western peoples, in their doctrines if not always in their practices. In this lies our greatest weapon, or in any case, we may hope, our indefeasible strength, against the totalitarian tyrannies. One must view with amazement the fact that any Jews have become communists. For though this intense stress on personality was also Stoic, and though early Christians helped themselves freely to Stoic doctrines, it has been in Judaism that this precious value has persisted most fully, and it is from this ancient source that the two hundred and fifty-odd Christian sects still nourish themselves.

In that, then, I find one of the deepest influences of the Bible on me. With all its ignorance, moral obtuseness and obsolete theological dogmas, our Western world continues to rest on moral choice. There is, as Van Wyck Brooks has pointed out in a recent luminous book, a widspread tendency to reject the *open society,* which has made this country great, and return to the *closed* society, that is, to a society in which the mind is governed by political or religious dogmas. The ancient Hebrews had commandments and rules and laws but *choice* was always the privilege of the individual. The notion of original sin, which Christians took not from Judaism but from the Orphics, and to which, lamenting, some of our contemporary writers have returned, is in my opinion utterly despicable. No more abhorrent doctrine than original depravity has ever been conceived. It is completely alien to Jewish thought and to the Bible, even though Christians use the Garden parable to give it divine sanction.

Hatred of tyrants and tyrannies and of the closed society I must have taken largely, at an impressionable age, from certain Biblical verses. From the Bible even more than from my mother, a stern and unbending Puritan, I got my extreme moral earnestness. I say it is extreme because a number of my more thoughtful critics have found it so. But any child and youth as influenced as I was by that book, who lives in a terrifying region that enhanced its gloomier aspects, could hardly grow up with much lightness of step or gayety of soul. For too many years I was a solemn, earnest and dedicated man.

And it follows that such sense of humor as I have is chiefly ironic. The lightness that plays over some people, touching them with graciousness, cloaking them with an atmosphere of tolerance and good humor, seldom touched me in my earlier years, and too often deserts me now. For me, life has been earnest if not always real!

My many early readings of the Bible developed in me a pathological sense of sin and of evil in the world, and of the brutality, not of women but of men. They developed in me a chronic pessimism; and though I reject such philosophies as Sartre's, I do perceive with Abrahams that "Reason must always leave God as unknowable." I haven't the faith to know him. It is not for nothing that Ecclesiastes is of all books in world literature the one I have read oftenest, or Job's question the one that seems to me most completely unanswerable. That the wicked prosper in both fortune and fellowship, while the good are not even loved, much less publicized, is still the riddle for any person who understands that mankind's schizophrenia has enthroned and hallowed the Devil. What else but this were the Biblical prophets thundering against?

All of which is to say that the Bible has had on me a tremendous influence for both good and ill. Whether there has been more of the one than of the other I shall never know. I have been fond of Vaughan's words, "There is in God a deep and dazzling darkness"; but at the same time only the weariest cynic can read the Bible and not perceive that there is also a great deal of light. Yet there have been great scholars who have found no light in it. They miss, I think, the important fact that the Hebrews were indeed, if not a unique at least a singular and peculiar people. Their spiritual leaders were solemnly and tirelessly preoccupied, not only with the relations of man to man which absorbed the interest of most peoples, but also with the relations of man to the universe. They were preoccupied with the thing called evil, when evil was not even a word in the vocabulary of some peoples. They were preoccupied with what they called righteousness, which, though sometimes suffocated in its elaborate apparatus of ritual, meant essentially good deeds. In defense of what they took to be the right way of life they had a capacity for suffering and self-immolation that has been quite without parallel.

Such is a part of what the Bible meant to me in my formative years. Today, after having read so many hundreds of learned books about it, I see it as a collection of fetishes, superstitions, legends, parables, poems, songs, prayers, moral apothegms, with such a richness of symbolism throughout that a myriad of books and at least one Harvard doctoral thesis have been devoted to it. Those who read the Bible literally, as nearly all Christians do, cannot hope to understand it at all. And I perceive, as Briffault has pointed out, that the fact that it was Judaism "which ultimately imposed itself upon the Western world, is perhaps not unconnected with the natural tendency to obliterate the last traces of matriarchal society." But men would have done that, granted the power, if the Bible had never been written: as Margaret Mead has recently said, mankind's failure to *institutionalize* those virtues more richly invested in women is the curse of life today.

If we believe with Thoreau that the "cost of a thing is the amount of what I will call life which is required to be exchanged for it" we must admit that the Bible has cost more than any other thing created by the mind and conscience of men. For good or for evil it has more than any other thing made us what we are in the Western world today. But who would undo the evil it has done if he must also forsake the good? Would anyone throw away the crypticism of Leviticus — "ye shall not eat anything with the blood" — if he must throw away the 42nd chapter of Isaiah — "To open the blind eyes, to bring out the prisoners from the prison, and them that sit in darkness out of the prison house"? Because such sentiments are common place now shall we forget how incredibly enlightened they were in Isaiah's time? Who would expunge "Thou shalt not suffer a witch to live," a so-called commandment that produced untold agony and horror upon Christians by Christians, if he must lose any one of a hundred brilliant things in Ecclesiasties, such as the first verse of the 4th chapter, "So I returned, and considered all the oppressions that are done under the sun: and behold the tears of such as were oppressed, and they had no comforter"? Who would sacrifice the tender parable of Ruth or of Hosea for the privilege of striking out a few passages that use a blunt language which offends our modern delicate ears?

We should, I think we must, accept the Bible humbly as the noblest effort of our ancient forebears to come to terms with the problem of evil and to overthrow it; and in the present, when the same old problem threatens to overturn our world, many of its pages and many of its beautiful parables still speak to us with a clear strong voice if we would only listen. For when we reject those parts no longer applicable we do not discredit those truths which, if not eternal, are still as eternal as any that man has uttered.

E. E. HOFFMAN

☆

BILLION DOLLAR CHECK RACKET

☆

Printed in U.S.A.

RENAY PUBLISHING CO.
P. O. BOX 22
TARZANA, CALIFORNIA
91356

SECOND EDITION, REVISED

Library of Congress Number:
HG1696.H6   332.9   62-16034

Copyright, 1964, by E. E. Hoffman
Published by Renay Publishing Co.
P. O. Box 22
Tarzana, California
91356

This book is dedicated to all law enforcement agencies, who should be getting more cooperation from the check cashing and check writing public.

CONTENTS

FORGERY IS BIG BUSINESS

TOO MANY businessmen have made up their minds that forged checks are just part of being in business. A forged check for ten dollars is a net loss representing one hundred dollars gross business. The forgery racket is doing one billion dollars worth of business this year. To the businessmen of the United States that will represent ten billion dollars gross business disappearing out of their pockets into the professional check artist's pocket and the amateur forger's too.

If I asked you to show me the uncollected, forged checks the bank has returned to you during the last six months could you find them? Although you gave your hard earned money for these pieces of paper, your bad checks are probably gathering dust in a desk drawer.

Perhaps you're resigned to your fate. If so, you might as well close this book right now. You don't need this book if you've decided to support the bad check artists.

But if you're ready to stop the spiralling bad check losses, this is the book for you. The more you know about the check artist the better your chances are of keeping him out of your pocket.

The businessman always has one eye looking for new customers; but he'd better keep both eyes wide-open when the new customer turns out to be a check forger. Supermarkets get thirty percent of the check forger's business. Holding down the number two spot on the popularity poll of the forger are department stores with twenty-one percent of his business. Gas stations and taverns run a close third with each walking away with thirteen percent of the forger's business. Ranking fourth, with nine percent, is the independent grocer. Liquor stores get five percent of the forger's business; drug stores about four percent; and banks, hotels and hardware stores share three percent. He cashes two percent of his bad checks in restaurants.

Don't feel hurt if you've been left out. This is one customer you don't need. By the time you finish this book you will be able to recognize him if he does pay you a visit.

Don't think that if you are not a businessman it can't affect the individual person that is not in business. Now that banks are spending a great deal of advertising beckoning people to open checking accounts it could just as well be you. Many times an individual will say, "I don't have enough money in the bank to worry about." Remember you may deposit $200.00 or even $100.00 to your checking account and write $80.00 in checks but until those checks clear your bank you still have $100.00 or $200.00 in the bank which is what forgers are interested in.

Forgery is known as the *silent crime* because the forger stays away from violence whenever possible. The only gun he needs is his pen. Many businessmen have suffered from this powerful weapon. In a recent newspaper article a parole officer was quoted as saying, "When we let a forger out on parole and he passes another bad check, it isn't too alarming. We're pretty certain he'll never hurt anybody." It is my opinion that if this parole officer were to have a check forged on his account two or three times a year he would take a different attitude.

It seems as if everybody is trying to get into the forgery

racket. At the moment only thirty-five percent of the business is being handled by professional check artists. The amateur forger today comes from every walk of life, every age group and sometimes takes in entire family groups. You can't pick up a newspaper today without reading about another forgery ring being apprehended or the police are looking for a young man, an old man, or a woman with three children for cashing forged checks. It's become routine news and you hardly take the time to read the stories. Take the time. Forgers are clever and they keep coming up with a slightly new switch to get their hands on your money. Learn these switches on the forgery racket as soon as they happen, so you won't fall into the same trap.

The upswing in forgery has made it a national problem. More money is lost each year from forgery and bank holdups than the combined fire losses in the United States and Canada. Only one person can halt this upward swing. It isn't the police officer nor is it the postal inspector. The only person who can call a halt to this racket is the individual businessman. The way he's going to stop the flow of his money into the pockets of the forger is by learning as much about forgery and checks as the forger knows. The businessman must learn *when* to say, "No, I'm sorry but I can't cash your check."

With a cautious, but friendly attitude and an honest appraisal of every check and its casher, the businessman can reduce his chances of taking a bad check. Some businessmen have found an effective use for bad checks on which they have the full history and know they'll never collect. In a prominent spot near the cash register, they place a bulletin board with a sign stating, "This is why we cannot cash checks for strangers." On the bulletin board the businessmen place the bad checks they know are dead issues. If you decide to use the bulletin board, make sure you use checks that are beyond recovery. Otherwise, it might prove embarrassing if

11

an honest customer came in to pay for an accidental checking error and discovered his check on your bulletin board. You could be involved in a lawsuit.

The one thought every businessman should bring to the attention of his customers is the fact that every time he cashes another bad check, this will be reflected in his profit margin. The good customer usually helps him balance his losses by paying higher prices.

CAN YOU AFFORD TO CONTRIBUTE?

CAN YOUR business afford to contribute to the *Billion Dollar Forgery Fund?* No business can. But every day thousands and thousands are making a contribution to this fund, supporting our growing army of amateur and professional check artists.

In talking to the head cashier of one of the largest chain stores in the country, I was told that when he talked to some of the managers of their stores and called attention to the fact that their check losses were up thirty percent over the preceding six months, he was told by one of the managers that the sales were up also. With an attitude like that, the check artist will always make a better living than the manager of the store, without the ever-present headaches and aggravation.

I'm going to show you how you can be sure you won't be contributing to these criminals. In my travels and in lectures on bad checks, I have cashed hundreds and hundreds of bad and altered checks with absolutely no trouble at all. After making my points with the actual cash I obtained with these checks, I naturally *returned the money to the surprised victims.* I can assure you no one else is going to return the money he receives for a bad check. I'll show you how to keep your money instead of contributing to the biggest racket in the United States today.

13

A check is only a piece of paper until it's cleared at the bank. You think twice before you give friends credit. Think three or four times before you give credit to strangers. In reality that's what you're doing when you cash a check for anyone. *You're allowing him credit until his check clears the bank.* If you insist upon running a credit organization for strangers, you may still remain in business, if you learn how to handle your checks.

When a stranger hands you a check and smiling tells you a very funny story about how his car broke down just outside your store, and he had to have it towed to a nearby garage, so he missed getting to the bank before it closed, and would you be kind enough to cash this check so he can pay for the items he's picked out and have enough left over to pay to have the car fixed . . . Well, the story goes on and on until you've cashed the check. Nine times out of ten, you've made a mistake.

Check artists and confidence men always have stories to tell, and usually the stories are much better than this one. There are several loopholes in the story you just read. Can you spot them? Well, nobody considers a flat tire a funny story. Can you remember the last time a car broke down in front of the store? And if he's having his car fixed, why doesn't the garage man cash his check? Any time an "entertaining talker" tells a story as he waits for you to okay his check, pay attention to what he's saying. You may pick up a clue that will nudge your suspicions.

Ask questions as soon as you notice misspelled words or signatures. One elderly check artist became known as "Mr. Ninety" because he liked to make out checks for ninety dollars. He was caught because he never learned there's an "e" in the word "ninety." Your suspicions should be aroused when a stranger hands you an illegible check. The check you can't read may be troublesome, so immediately begin asking questions.

Beware of checks with rubber-stamped company names. A company usually has its own payroll and business checks imprinted, using a regular bank cut.

Start asking questions if the check you're given is a large company draft written on a counter check form. Particularly be wary if the counter check is "doctored up" with a check protector and rubber stamp.

Is the check you're about to cash really a check? Make sure it's not a voucher or merchandise order.

Don't accept a post-dated check and don't agree to hold a check for any reason. Give the check back to the stranger if he states he must make a deposit to cover it. Let him use the cash he was going to deposit to cover his purchase. *Make it a firm business rule not to accept a personal check for more than the amount of the purchase.*

It is possible to cut down a great deal of this loss. The best way to take the profit out of the forgery racket is by limiting the amount of cash that you will pay out on a check. Once the check artist knows that he cannot get cash and merchandise, he will stop calling on you. They are not interested in the merchandise that they have to buy, *the big object is to see how much cash they can take out of your till.*

If the stranger has obviously been drinking, don't cash his check. Ask him to come back tomorrow or discover you don't have enough cash on hand.

Under no circumstances return the check to the passer after approving it or you may start finding your approval signature or notation appearing on checks you've never seen. Where a manager of a bank had O.K.'d a check for a stranger then handed the check back to the stranger, the stranger would stop at the counter and alter the check to a larger amount, then present it to the teller for payment. Now, most bank personnel will hand the check to the teller and point the customer out, should he have to get in line. This is a much safer procedure for the bank.

Bad checks are most frequently passed on week-ends and holidays when banks are closed. If you have a doubt and the banks are open, use their services to double-check a check. They don't want you to get stuck with a bad check and are glad to be of help. If a bad check is from out-of-state, it's usually hard to prosecute. Calling a telephone number on a check is no proof the check is legitimate. The check passer's accomplice will undoubtedly answer the phone. However, *if the telephone number that was originally printed on the check has been obliterated, and a rubber stamp number put in its place, then verify the firm on which the check has been drawn by calling information and asking for the phone number.* Professional check passers will usually have a new phone number stamped on the check which is a pay station where they will have an accomplice answer the phone representing the firm name on which his partner is passing the checks. This seems to satisfy most businessmen that the check is good, as the man answering the phone speaks very highly of the man who is in the store.

If you call the police, delay the stranger without arousing his suspicions. If he leaves before the police arrive, try to get his license number or his means and route of departure. It's practically impossible to get a conviction on a bad check issued for ten dollars or less, since it's a misdemeanor. Regardless, report all the information you have to the police about every bad check you receive.

Whenever anyone asks you to cash a check, whether he is a steady customer or a stranger, remember a check is not legal tender. You are doing the customer a favor. As long as you maintain your friendly, interested attitude while asking questions about the check, you won't run the risk of losing your good customers. The confidence man or the check artist can't afford to give you the time to prove your suspicions. So these are the customers you'll be losing if you make it a practice not to hand out your money too quickly.

WHO IS DOING WHOM A FAVOR?

THE GREATEST mistake the businessman has made in recent years is allowing the public to put him on the offensive in terms of cashing checks. A businessman is afraid not to cash a check; he'd be financially better off if his attitude was just the reverse.

Only one thing can help him, and that's a cooperative advertising campaign by businessmen all over the country based on "WE'RE DOING YOU, THE PUBLIC, A FAVOR WHEN WE CASH YOUR CHECKS."

The customer now feels he's doing the businessman a favor by letting the businessman cash his checks. He's stopped carrying money, except a few coins to slip into a parking meter. In this day and age he doesn't need to carry money. He knows everyone wants to cash his checks.

In the Midwest a very successful supermarket found itself holding a stack of checks returned from the bank stamped "No Account," "Stolen," "Signature Irregular," "Account Closed," etc. The management decided to adopt a get-tough policy on cashing checks. All checks were now examined carefully, identifications were thoroughly inspected, and the management refused any check that seemed in any way a poor risk. Within days business began to fall off and a week later business had fallen twenty percent. This supermarket was forced to resume its easy-going check cashing policy and

17

decided it would at least be more fun to go broke with a store full of customers. The mistake that was made in this case was the change of policy without re-educating the customers to appreciate the reasons for the new policy. One good point to make with customers, when trying the new policy, is the fact that if it works, the customers will profit with new low prices. You must stress that you want to share your profits with your customers rather than your losses from bad checks. This is the approach that will bring you new customers. They'll want to take advantage of the new, low money-saving prices you offer, due to your protective business sense.

The two things a professional check artist objects to are being finger printed and photographed. Both of these devices have been attempted to cut down the widespread increase in the passing of bad checks. Naturally, the check artist objects. The big surprise has been the resistance of the general public. There is nothing wrong with the principle of either photographing or finger printing a person who wants to cash a check. But people have not been educated to accept it. This is a public relations job that businessmen everywhere must share. The public feels both devices put it in the same boat as the criminal. The average individual resents being put in this position. If we're to slow down the rising billion-dollar bad check business we're going to have to change their attitude.

Many stores are adopting a card system where they will have the customer fill out a questionnaire similar to a credit statement. Then they assign him an account number. Should he want to cash a check, thereafter, he merely shows the card given him which states that he has already the filed information needed, and there is no delay. This is a printed card showing the store number that issued it.

Businessmen must get their message across to the general public. What would your reaction be to a stranger who rings your doorbell and asks you to cash a check for him? Would you comply with his request? They must also get their message across to the professional check artist whose success and overconfidence has become alarming. The check artist must learn that businessmen will no longer consider bad checks a necessary evil in running a business.

The frightening overconfidence of today's check artist can best be shown in an actual case that happened to the owner of a hardware store. A customer came in, purchased $22.00 in merchandise and gave the store owner a payroll check worth $88.00. The customer's identification was satisfactory and the check seemed to be in order so the store owner gladly cashed the check. The customer was busily chattering away about why he was getting these supplies. He and his wife had just found a new apartment. The owner invited the new customer to bring his wife into the store sometime. The customer returned and said he had been so busy talking he'd forgotten to pick up his trading stamps. The store owner apologized for having forgotten to give the stamps to him, did so, and the customer left. Less than a week later this merchant received a notice from his bank that they were charging back an $88.00 item. After a little thought he remembered about the man who came in with a check stolen from one of the leading contractors in his town, and was a forgery. A telephone call would have saved him this loss and his trading stamps. He told me that he would have rather been held up with a gun. I then reminded him that the check artist would never have come back for his stamps if he had been an "honest" hold-up man.

NON SUFFICIENT FUNDS

"N.S.F." STAMPED ON a check and returned to you by your bank means one of two things. Either the money you paid out for that check will be tied up for a while; or you'll never collect it. The only protection the businessman has against "N.S.F." checks is a firmer bank policy and customer education.

The number of "N.S.F." checks returned varies with the section of the country, the bank, and the bank's policy. More checks are returned by banks in the West, particularly California, then in the East. Many California banks run as high as 150 checks returned daily marked "N.S.F." This means 150 people or businesses will be denied the use of money legally and morally theirs. These "N.S.F." checks cover either money or merchandise given to the makers of the check in good faith. Some of these checks may have been written in good faith and the makers may have honestly believed they had funds to cover them. But when a bank stamps "Non Sufficient Funds" on 150 checks daily, these are not all honest mistakes. A person who knowingly cashes a check he hasn't the funds to cover is morally wrong. It's time both the businessman and the bank made this customer aware of it. The bank does offer token resistance by charging a penalty fee of $1.50 to $2.00

to the "N.S.F." check writer's account. The person who is deliberately carrying out this type of fraud willingly pays this minor penalty for the use of the funds which are not his. It's the bank's responsibility and duty to take off its kid gloves with the customers who specialize in this practice. The businessman who finds repeated "N.S.F." checks being returned from the same bank and the same customers, must take off his kid gloves with both the particular bank and the particular customers. The businessman must remind the bank of its responsibilities which include the type of customer it allows to use its services. Likewise, the businessman must refuse to cash checks for customers addicted to the "N.S.F." habit. If the businessman doesn't do this, he'll be running a loan office for people without collateral.

The bank must take a firm position in its dealings with customers who have fallen into the habit of cashing checks without the funds to cover them. With many of these people it has become a bad habit that they can't kick. The only solution with these people is for the bank to cancel their accounts. They can only give the bank a bad reputation and are unfair to the businessman trying to make a living.

Unfortunately, everyone is too easy on the culprit who practices this deception. The one place where the honest error can be separated from the habit-formed repeater is at the bank. The bank can raise the penalties on repeaters. All offenders should be called into the bank and made aware of their responsibilities to the community and to the bank. A limit should be placed on the number of "N.S.F." checks the bank will accept from any one account. When that limit is reached, the account should be closed. The bank that loses a few of these customers in a move to protect the community it has promised to serve, stands to gain new respect and appreciation from businessmen everywhere.

Many merchants have discouraged customers from issuing Non Sufficient Funds checks by charging a $1.00 fee for any check returned stamped "N.S.F.". This fee has nothing to do with bank charges.

The most important thing to remember about checks stamped "N.S.F." is that you can only deposit them two times. So you have two strikes against you when the check is returned stamped "N.S.F.". When you deposit the check the second time and the customer still doesn't have the funds to cover the check, you've had your third strike and you're out. Before you go for the third strike, make sure the customer has enough money in the bank to cover your check. One method of getting information you need is to call the bank and lay your cards on the table. Usually, the bank will cooperate and give you the information as to whether or not the customer now has the funds on deposit to cover the check. If the answer is "Yes", run, don't walk to the customer's bank and cash that check. Now if you have a problem in obtaining the information from the bank, here's one sure method of getting the information immediately. Call the bank and ask for the bookkeeper who handles the check writer's account. Tell the bookkeeper you have a C.O.D., and ask if there's enough money in the person's account to cover it. If there is, again, don't walk, run to the customer's bank and cash that check. Don't deposit the check in your own bank. By the time the check would arrive at the customer's bank, his funds may once again be depleted. If the check has been returned twice, you will be forced to track down the customer and get him to issue a new check. Of course, the direct approach is always the best. As soon as you receive a check stamped "N.S.F.", contact the check writer. Insist that he bring the cash to you to cover the check. Usually he'll want you to redeposit the check. But if you're insistent, he'll arrive at your place of business with the cash. As long as you're holding a "N.S.F." check, that particular customer is holding your hard-earned dollars. You've already done the customer an initial favor by cashing his check. Let him return the favor by bringing the cash to you. <u>The police are not a collection agency</u> so don't expect them to collect for you. If you insist upon running a credit agency, you must be the collector.

THE FORGED SIGNATURE

IDENTIFICATION papers are obtained by the forger by robbing mail boxes, stealing wallets, stealing from offices and stealing from private homes. The easiest identification to obtain without stealing are fish and game permits, and temporary driver's licenses. Once he has his hand on any sort of identification papers, the forger only needs to be able to sign a name and he's in business. It's a business that's too easy to start. The careful businessman can make it tougher for the new forger to start his business.

Your safest protection in keeping both the amateur forger and the professional check artist out of your bank account is to use a clear-cut, legible signature. Stay away from elegant flourishes, as shown in Figure 1.

Many bookkeepers are happy that banks are using magnetic account numbers. This of course takes out the guessing as to whom to charge the check to, even though they cannot decipher the signature.

Many businessmen have made this remark, "No one can forge my signature, because no one can read it!" If you've ever made that statement, don't be proud of it. If no one can read your signature, how do you expect your bank to know when not to pay out your money?

FIGURE 1

This is the easiest type of signature to forge. The clear-cut signature is the most difficult.

There are several methods used in forging signatures. The professional check artist favors the muscle forgery or the reverse writing method. In this operation the signature that is to be forged is turned upside down and copied backwards. In most cases he will not even look at the name he is going to forge until the forgery has been completed. With this method the forger relies on the muscles of his forearm to get away from his own style of handwriting and really makes a series of lines and whirls. It gets him away from his natural style of writing certain letters. Figure 2 shows the muscle forger in action.

A factory employee used a unique method of forging his employer's checks. While the bookkeeper was at lunch, he stole six checks from the back of the checkbook she carelessly left on her desk. By tapeing his regular pay check to the bottom of a piece of glass, he then put one stolen check on the top, lining up the signature line. Placing the glass over a small empty box which contained a large lit bulb enabled him to see through both checks. He then traced the visible signature. His downfall came as a result of the police investigating this case. They did detect several sets of identical signatures. The forger should have known that nobody can sign his name exactly the same twice. Although the stolen checks were made out to other persons, his regular paycheck bore the exact markings of the forged instruments.

The businessman who stands a chance of escaping the forged signature and the bad check is the *careful* businessman who protects his banking signature. By checking and double-checking the use of his banking signature, the businessman can stay out of forger's hands.

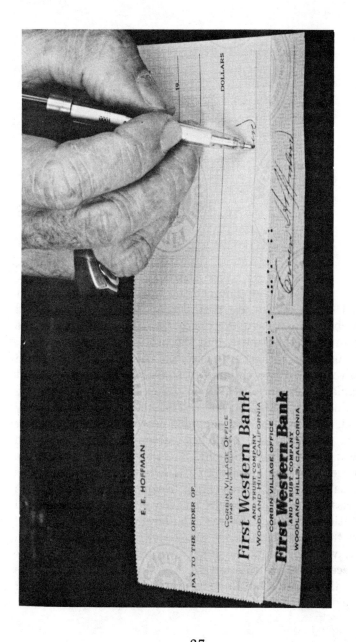

FIGURE 2

In order to master the characteristics of a writing style, professionals make a picture of the signature by tracing it upside down and backwards.

27

THREE TYPES OF CHECK ARTISTS

AMATEUR

Law enforcement agencies will admit that not all check artists are professionals. In my surveys and research, I would say there are three distinct types: the amateur, the opportunist, and the professional.

Let us start with the amateur in the case of a divorced woman who had two children to support without the benefit of regular allotment checks from her ex-husband. Her household bills were getting bigger, and in order to keep her family in food, she would go to a shopping center where she was not known, buy what she needed as necessities, and pay with a check for the exact amount. She told me that as long as the check was not more than the actual purchase, she was never asked for any identification. Keeping a list of the stores she passed the bogus checks on, she intended to make full restitution as soon as she was able; however, she was arrested before this came to pass.

The way our economy is set up today, accepting checks is a necessity. Nevertheless, ask a few questions of strangers even if there is no cash to be returned. Merchandise given for a piece of paper is still an investment for you.

28

OPPORTUNIST

The opportunist could be the most honest employee you have in your business. His operation usually starts with temptation. Many employers tempt their employees without knowing it. They take for granted that everyone is honest. Let us take, for example, the case of a doctor who lost several thousand dollars due to his habit of banking. When making up his deposit slip, he would stamp most of the checks received from his patients with a rubber stamp "FOR DEPOSIT ONLY". If he were short of cash, he would endorse one or two checks in longhand and cash them while depositing the rest to his account. As his practice grew, he hired a bookkeeper to handle office routine. He also instructed the bank clerk to cash any checks she might bring, just as he had done in the past. As time went on, an audit disclosed that the bookkeeper had been forging the doctor's name to the back of the checks without his permission, and keeping the cash for herself. He was completely unaware of her embezzling as she would open all incoming mail.

Another case where the opportunist came to light was when an auditor wanted the better things in life he could not afford on his salary. Although he was not an eligible signer of the firm's checks, he did have complete control of the checkbook. He started out in grand style by forging checks in large amounts. When his acts were finally discovered, the bank admitted that the forgeries were very poor and that restitution would be made if the owners would sign a complaint and sign the necessary statements. The auditor informed them that if they chose to prosecute, he would expose some shady financial dealings they were involved in of which he was aware. The owners did not press for prosecution nor did the bank reimburse them for the forged checks.

PROFESSIONAL

The professional is the check artist you hear the least about. He is the big money operator and, usually, cases of this sort are kept out of the papers, for face-saving tactics. Banks are usually involved in these cases and do not like the publicity.

In this particular case banks and business firms contributed $470,000. in a ten month period, to a two-man operation. The operators first act was to break into an office of a good sized firm and steal several blank checks and a current bank statement. The bank statement acted as a financial guide, while the cancelled checks had a specimen of the handwriting and signature. The next morning one man would cut the phone wires leading into the office at the same time as the other was presenting a check to be cashed at the bank. Since the check was for a large amount, the manager would try calling the firm to verify the check's authenticity. After getting a busy signal for ten minutes, the forger would offer to drive the bank manager to this place of business for verification. Figuring that the check must be good, the manager OK'd the check for cashing.

Many businessmen will remember a little old lady, gray-haired, who called on their places of business with a check for $1.00. She told them that she was going downtown to get her old age pension check; inasmuch as she did not have any change for bus fare, she asked if they would do her the favor of cashing a personal check for $1.00. The check was made out to cash. Very few business men turned her down. The police, from the complaints they received, estimate that she was good for at least $20 to $30 a day. Small amounts, yes, but they did add up. In talking to lawmen all over the country, I asked them the following question, "If you were going to enter a life of crime, what phase would you pick?". The answer was always, "CHECKS."

30

WHO IS LIABLE for a forged check? It's a good question that has brought many legal battles. Any time there is trouble with a check, it presents a problem just as does a patient in a doctor's office. Every one is different. (See cases involved, Figures 3, 3A and 3B.)

A bank is merely an agent in handling your funds. If the signature does not resemble the specimen you have on file with the bank and the check is paid out of your funds, you can hold the bank responsible for the item. If, however, the signature is an excellent forgery, you may have to sue the bank. No manager of a bank will admit the bank is liable for a forgery. I have never been able to get a bank manager to *sign a statement to that effect.*

If you have a forged check the bank deducted from your account, this is the procedure you should follow:

Fill out a statement of proof of loss and have it notarized.

Give it to the bank manager and he will send it to the main office, along with a specimen of your bank signature. From the main office the forged check and signature specimen are sent to a crime laboratory and analyzed by a handwriting expert. If the handwriting expert has any doubt about the check being forged, *the bank can refuse to reimburse you.*

31

COURT DECISIONS IN LITIGATED CASES IN-
VOLVING BANK RESPONSIBILITY FOR FORGERY
AND/OR ALTERATION OF CHECKS

Amount	Cause	Disposition	Title and Reference
$ 2800.00	Forgery	Bank won	Armour & Co. vs. Green County State Bk. U. S. Circuit Court of Appeals - 112 Fed. R. 630
1800.00	Forgery	Maker won	United Security L. I. Trust Co. vs. Central National Bank Penn. 40 Atl. R. 97
3000.00	Forgery	Bank won	Marks vs. Anchor Savings Bank Penn. 97 Atl. R. 399
1450.00	Forgery	Bank won	Connors vs. Old Forge Discount Bank Penn. 91 Atl. R. 210
4000.00	Forgery	Bank won	Lesley vs. Ewing Penn. 93 Atl. R. 875
141.00	Forgery	Bank won	Findley vs. Corn Exchange National Bank Illinois 166, Ill. App. 57
52500.00	Forgery	Bank won	American Hominy Company vs. Milliken National Bank U.S. Circuit Court of Appeals, 273 Fed. R. 550
1250.00	Forgery	Bank won	U. S. vs. National Exchange Bank U. S. Circuit Court of Appeals, 45 Fed. R. 163
13000.00	Forgery	Bank won	North British & Mercantile Insurance Co. vs. Merchants National Bank New York 161 App. Div. 341
3100.00	Forgery	Bank won	Pannonia Bldg. & Loan Association vs. West Side Trust Co. N. Jersey Los. Atl. Rep. 240
122.13	Forgery	Bank won	Weisberger vs. Barberton Savings Bank Ohio 95 N. E. Rep. 379
16000.00	Forgery	Maker won	Los Angeles Investment Co. vs. Home Savings Bank California 180 Cal. 601
18500.00	Forgery and Alterations	Bank won	Union Tool Works vs. F. & M. National Bank Calif. 66 Cal. Dec. 317
135 drafts	Forgery	Bank won	Bartlett vs. First National Bank Illinois 93 N. E. Rep. 337
18400.00	Forgery	Bank won	Snyder vs. Corn Exchange Bank Penn. 70 Atl. Rep. 876
3600.00	Forgery	Bank won	Prudential Insurance Co. vs. National Bank of Commerce New York 130 N. Y. Supp. 227 N. Y. 610
1000.00	Forgery	Bank won	Annel vs. Chase National Bank New York 196 App. Div. 632
1076.25	Forgery	Bank won	Murray vs. R. E. Title Insurance & Trust Company Penn. 39 Sup. Ct. Rep. 438
480.00	Forged Sig.	Bank won	M. M. McKeen & Company vs. Boatmen's Bank Missouri 74 Mo. App. 281
4000.00	Forged Sig.	Bank won	California Vegetable Union vs. Crocker National Bank Calif. 57 Cal. App. 743-174 Pac. R. 920
13000.00	Forged Sig.	Bank won	Meyers vs. Southwestern National bank Penn. 193 Penn. U. R. 1-rr Atl. R. 97 R. 280
90 checks	Forged Sig.	Bank won	McNeely Company vs. Bank of North America Penn. 70 Atl. R. 891
63000.00	Forged Certif.	Maker won	Continental Bank vs. Bank of Commonwealth New York 50 N. Y. 583

FIGURE 3

Amount	Cause	Disposition	Title and Reference
$ 275.00	Forged Sig.	Bank won	Neal vs. First National Bank Indiana 60 N. E. Rep. 164
1000.00	Forged Sig.	Bank won	Weinstein vs. National Bank of Jefferson Texas 5 Am. St. R. 23
35000.00	Forged Sig.	Bank won	Morgan vs. U. S. Mortgage & Trust Company New York 208 N. Y. 218
853.00	Forged Sig.	Bank won	Israel vs. State National Bank Louisiana 50 So. R. 783
1700.00	Forged Sig.	Bank won	Deferiet vs. Bank of America Louisiana 50 So. R. 8 Am. Rep. 597
1000.00	Forged Sig.	Maker won	Kenneth Investment Co. vs. National Bank of Replc. Missouri 77 S. W. Rep. 1002
3500.00	Forged Sig.	Maker won	Denhigh vs. National Bank Washington 102 Wash. 546
75000.00	Forged Sig.	Bank won	Shattuck vs. Guardian Trust Company New York 130 N. Y. Supp. 658
8875.00	Forged Sig., Alt.	Bank won	Chas. Harley Co. vs. American National Bank California Cal. Superior Ct. S. F. Co. No. 116,355
148.00	Forged Sig.	Maker won	First National Bank vs. U. S. National Bank Oregon 197 Pac. Rep. 547
500.00	Forged Sig.	Bank won	First National Bank vs. Allen Alabama 14 So. R. 335
5150.00	Raising	Bank won	Hammerschlag Mfg. Co. vs. Importers & Traders National Bank U. S. Ct. 262 Fed. (N. Y.) R. 266
10000.00	Raising	Bank won	Leather Mfrs. Bank vs. Morgan U. S. Supreme Court 117, U. S. 96
6500.00	Raising and Forgery of payee line	Bank won	Otis Elevator Co. vs. First National Bank Calif. 163 Cal. 31
31000.00	Raising and Alt. of payee line	Maker won	National Dredging Co. vs. Farmer's Bank Delaware 22 Del. 580, 69, App. R. 607
2600.00	Raising of Amount	Bank won	First National Bank vs. Richmond Elevator Company Virginia 106 Va. 347 56 S. E. Rep. 152
2400.00	Raising and Alteration	Bank won	Critten vs. Chemical National Bank New York 171 N. Y. 219
	Alteration of payee's line	Bank won	Dana vs. National Bank of Republic Massachusetts 132 Mass. 156
124.00	Alteration of Amount	Bank won	Jones & Co. vs. Bank of Horatio 143 S. W. Rep. 1060
196.76	Alteration of date and amount	Bank won	Mitchell vs. Security Bank New York 85 N. Y. Misc. 360
4000.00	Raising	Bank won	Timbel vs. Garfield National Bank New York 121 App. Div. 870
10495.00	Raising	Bank won	Glassell Development Co. vs. Citizens Na- tional Bank Calif. 66 Cal. Dec. 27

NOTE   45 CASES
            35 INVOLVE FORGERY and/or Alteration
            10 INVOLVE ALTERATION only

BANK WON IN 38 CASES
MAKER WON IN 7 CASES

SOME CASES IN LITIGATION for from 6 to 9 YEARS

FIGURE 3A

33

Your next step is to start a lawsuit. This may result in months of litigation. In some cases, to maintain good relations, the bank will reimburse the customer even when there is a doubt. Some banks utilize the services of their bonding companies to follow through check forgery disputes. In some states this is mandatory.

Examine your bank statement and cancelled checks carefully. *You are responsible* if you fail to notify the bank that you have found a forged check among your cancelled checks. Otherwise, the bank is not liable for any similar forgeries occurring between the time the first cancelled forged check was returned to you with your bank statement and the time you reported the forgeries to the bank. This could be an expensive oversight.

I recall the case of a service station owner by the name of Mr. Gentry. One slow morning he'll remember for a long time, a man walked into the station and handed him two $100.00 bills. He had been a friend in years past, but had not seen Mr. Gentry for a few years. At one time he used to do odd jobs and help in doing various chores around the station. Many times he had the occasion to go to the bank to get change and make deposits for Mr. Gentry. Upon being asked what the money was for, he related a story that he had come back to town to get a job and settle down. In the meantime he had gone to visit a gambling parlor, and when his luck had run out he wrote two checks amounting to $200.00 on Mr. Gentry's account but later was able to recoup some of his losses. Since he was not able to get the checks back, he thought he would bring the cash. It was then that Mr. Gentry opened his bank statement which he had received a few days earlier and sure enough there were two checks. The signatures could have easily passed for genuine. He gave his friend a severe tongue-lashing and told him that the next time he did that he would report him to the police. The following month, when the statement was received, Mr.

LEGAL DECISIONS

THE U. S. SUPREME COURT — THE U. S. CIRCUIT COURT
THE COURT OF COMMON PLEAS AND OTHER AUTHORITIES ON
LAW HAVE RENDERED THE FOLLOWING DECISIONS . . . .

. . . "The maker of check is **obliged** to use all due diligence in protecting it; the omission to use the **most effectual protection** against alteration, is evidence of neglect, which renders him responsible for the fraudulent amount, the bank being responsible only for the apparent genuineness of the signature and ordinary care in paying a check." . . . .
. . . The appellee admitted that for the previous five years he knew of means used by bankers and merchants to prevent the raising of checks, but had not used any of them. — *Leather Manufacturers' Bank vs. Morgan, et al., 171 U. S.* ¶96. . . . .

. . . .
. . . The purport of this decision is that if the drawer of a check which was altered and paid neglected to use means easily obtainable, to protect his check from alteration, **the drawer** must stand the loss occasioned thereby.

The opinion of the court was delivered by Justice Harlan F. Stone of the Supreme Court of the United States.

———

"If, by any act or negligence on the part of the drawer, as by so carelessly writing the check as to render it easily open to material **alteration** without leaving evident traces of such alteration, the customer has furnished the opportunity for the fraud which has deceived the bank, he must suffer the just consequences of his carelessness by bearing the loss himself." . . .
. . . . — *Morse on Banks and Banking, Sec. 480; and Young vs. Grote, 4 Bing. 253.*

———

"The bank is not bound to know anything more than the drawer's signature, and in the absence of any circumstances which inflict injury upon another party there is no reason why the bank should not be reimbursed. Its certification of the check does not preclude it from showing an alteration, nor does its teller's declaration after he has examined it, and stated that it is right in every particular." . . . .
. . . . — *The Supreme Court of Illinois.*

"For clearly a bank has a right to demand some duties from its customers in such an important matter as protection from fraud, in a business where frauds of a particularly skillful and ingenious nature are continually in course of preparation." . . . . . .
. . . . — *Morse on Banks, 235.*

———

"The drawee can be held bound only to know the signature of the depositor, and **not the hand-writing of the body of the check,** the money paid in good faith and without negligence on an altered check, may be recovered by the bank." . . .
. . . . — *United States — Espey vs. Cincinnati Bank, 18 Wall (U. S.) 614.*

———

"A man signed checks for his wife's expenses while he is absent. His wife filled in a check for £ 51 and handed it to the clerk to get the cash. The clerk wrote in "hundred," changed the figures to correspond, using a different ink and a different handwriting. The court held that 'the difference in handwriting in the body of the check was not a matter of suspicion where neither of them were the hand of the signer.' " — *American and English Encyclopedia of Law, Vol. V, page 1075.*

———

"The maker of check is bound to use recognized safeguards in protecting his check against alteration, where an innocent holder may sustain loss." . . .
. . . . . . — *Daniel on Negotiable Instruments.*

———

Maxim of the Common Law

———

Where one of two innocent persons must suffer by the act of a third, he by whose negligence it happened must be the sufferer.

FIGURE 3B

Gentry opened it immediately and his ire was newly aroused. There were three checks payable to the same casino, which Mr. Gentry was sure he had not written. He immediately tried to get in touch with his ex-friend but found out he had left town again. He went to the bank and explained the past dealings to the manager. When the report came back from the main office he was told that inasmuch as he knew of the last months' forgeries, and did not report them, they felt that he should stand the entire loss. It cost him $875.00.

A depositor must report a forgery or a raised check after the return of the bank statement of such payment. Otherwise, the bank is in no way liable for payment. The time limit for such reports varies with different banks. Ask your bank as to its expiration date for such reports! Don't put off checking and doublechecking your bank statement and your cancelled checks.

LET'S TAKE a look at the last bank statement you received. You should have already examined it carefully. Right now let's concentrate on your signatures that have cleared the bank. (See Figure 4.) You won't find two signatures *exactly* the same in the last five hundred checks. Now put down that phone. This isn't the time to call the bank and file a complaint. It's virtually impossible to sign your name exactly the same way twice.

The "T" that may appear in your name looks the same as far as characteristics are concerned. A closer inspection will show you the top loop of one "T" may be large; on the next check it may be smaller. Your bank pays out your funds on a recognizable signature.

A thought to remember the next time you're about to scratch out your signature hurriedly on the bottom of a check, this is the recognizable signature that can remove one dollar or a thousand dollars from your bank account.

The key to your bank balance is your signature and it's up to you to protect it as carefully as you do your daily cash receipts.

You may smile and say, "It takes two signatures on every check that leaves our firm, so we're safe." Don't relax too soon. The check artist is usually a smooth operator who never

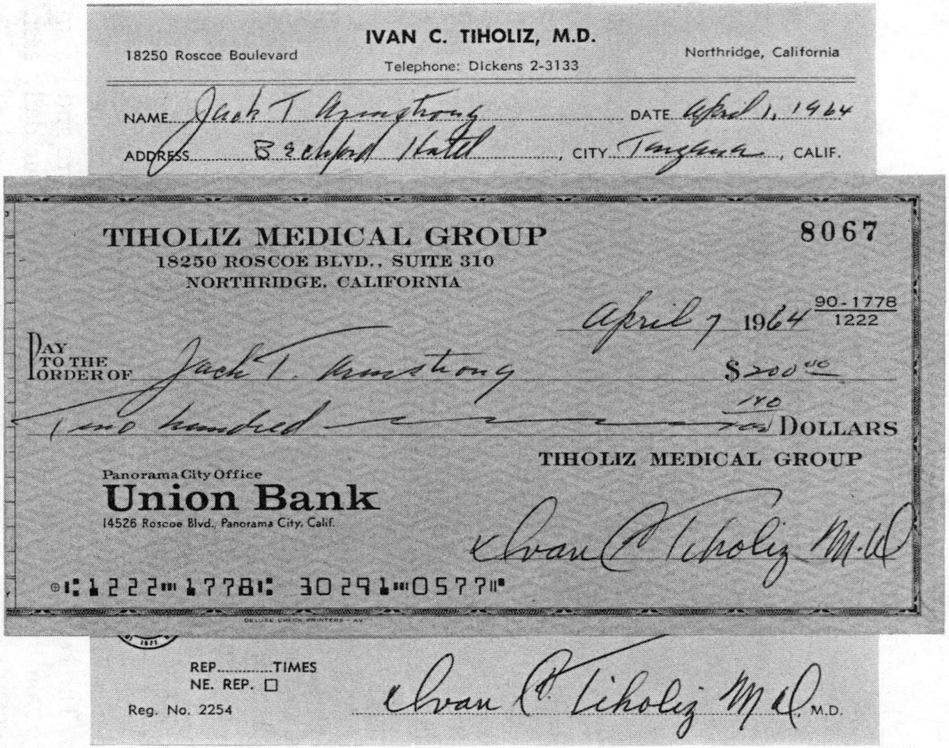

FIGURE 4

Medical men should never use the same signature on prescriptions as they use on checks.

gives his victim an even break. The professionals are always the finest confidence men in the criminal world. They know how to secure your signature or your signatures. I personally have used over one hundred methods in successfully obtaining authentic bank signatures.

Doctors are an easy prey for the professional forger. The forger makes an office visit as a patient. Probably he has already stolen some of the doctor's checks a week earlier. Many a doctor has found out the hard way that had he begun using a prescription signature different from the way he signed the checks, he would have been hundreds of dollars ahead. This is a good way to get a doctor's signature. The illness he feigns warrants a prescription and he happily pays for this office call. He walks out with the doctor's signature and very probably the doctor's bank balance.

A method I have personally used when planning a lecture for a particular organization is to visit the store of one of the members with a gift-wrapped package which contains an inexpensive pair of socks. I tell Mr. Andrews, my intended victim, that Mr. Borden (a fictitious dealer representing a manufacturer with whom I know he does business) asked me to deliver the package to him and would he please sign the attached card to show I had made delivery. Mr. Andrews' attention is on the gift and he signs his full signature on the card. As I leave Mr. Andrews' store, he is busily unwrapping the gift, completely unaware that I could be walking away with his total capital.

During my lecture for Mr. Andrews' organization, I contribute $100.00 in cash to the group's welfare fund and tell them the contribution is for the privilege of speaking to such a fine looking group. As soon as the applause dies down, I tell them the contribution really came from a favorite benefactor of theirs, Mr. Andrews. I then relate how I obtained Mr. Andrews' signature and cashed a counter check for $100.00, copying his signature from the card.

The full impact of the message I wanted to get across to the group begins to sink in. Every man at the meeting realizes I could have taken every penny Mr. Andrews had in his bank account with that very same signature. Besides a smaller bank account, Mr. Andrews, or any other businessman present, would have had one other memory . . . the inexpensive pair of socks I so carefully gift wrapped. (Later when Mr. Andrews' money was returned, he told me what really upset him was the socks weren't even the right size.)

No delivery man will refuse to leave a shipment, if you just initial the delivery slip. A complete signature, especially your bank signature, is not necessary. If Mr. Andrews had only initialed my receipt, I would have lost a pair of socks and lost the moral to my story of how careless we can be when we think we're getting something for nothing.

Your attorney, your bank, and your police department will all advise you to keep your banking signature out of the limelight as much as possible. You'll be taking a step in the right direction, if you use *one signature* for banking and *another* for general correspondence and other uses.

YOUR SIGNED CHECK IS A PRIZE

THE MOST VALUED prize to the professional check artist is getting his hands on your own check that bears your bank signature. All he has to do when he has this piece of paper in his hands is to increase the amount of the check. This check is as good as cash in his pocket.

That's why the check artist goes out of his way to find new methods of getting his hands on your signed checks. One method he uses is direct selling. Everyone likes a bargain and the professional check artist thrives on this knowlodge.

He will call on a garage and offer to leave merchandise with the owner on a consignment basis. This means no cash outlay to the garage owner. After the merchandise has been in stock for a week or two, the check artist's accomplice will stop in as a casual customer. He just happens to purchase a couple of the items that were put in on a so-called consignment deal. Needless to say, he appears to be very happy with his purchases. After a month has olapsed, the original salesman makes his repeat call and notes some of the items have been sold. If the garage owner offers to pay for the merchandise sold with a cash payment, the check artist will say he is not allowed to collect, explaining the payment should be sent to the office which is, in all cases, a temporary setup. Carefully he avoids using the word "check". He knows few businessmen will send cash through the mail.

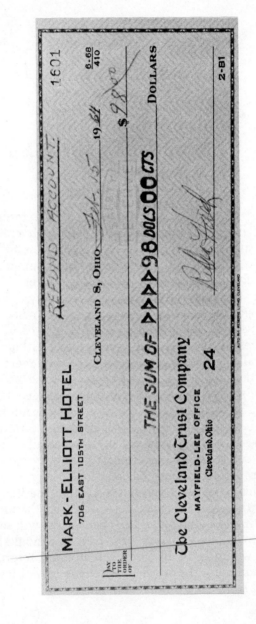

FIGURE 5

After: Could you legitimately question the amount? The signature is genuine.

42

FIGURE 6

Before: A legally signed check that any bank would honor. This is not a forgery.

43

The check artist loses a little money on the consignment deal, but he gets the prize he's after . . . the key to the garage owner's checking account, a signed check. The garage owner sometimes ends up by handing him a check on the spot. The check artist may have to wait until he receives it in the mail. Either way, he ends up with his prize.

This racket is worked in drug stores, independent food markets, record shops, stationery stores, dress shops, men's shops, linen shops, and any other independent small store. This racket plays on the vulnerability of the small store owner who wants to add more merchandise but cannot afford it. The consignment deal at no cost or investment appeals to the small merchant.

The racket used on hotels and motels is for the check artist to make a reservation for about a month in advance. For this he will leave a deposit in cash. In about two weeks he will write a letter to the hotel or motel explaining his plans have changed. He requests a refund since he cannot use the reservation. The unsuspecting reservation clerk will remit his deposit in the form of a check. This check bears the hotel or motel manager's genuine signature . . . which is the end of the rainbow to the check artist.

This racket is also worked successfully on businesses such as florists, bakeries, and apartment houses. Any type of business that accepts reservations or orders in advance is a possible victim of this racket.

There is a way of beating the professional check artist in both of these rackets. Set up a special bank account for checks covering small amounts you will be paying out to strangers. Then follow the same procedure that has proved helpful to the United States Post Office in preparing its postal money orders.

When you have your checks for this special bank account imprinted, *print on each of these checks a maximum value*. Your bank will not honor any check raised to more than that

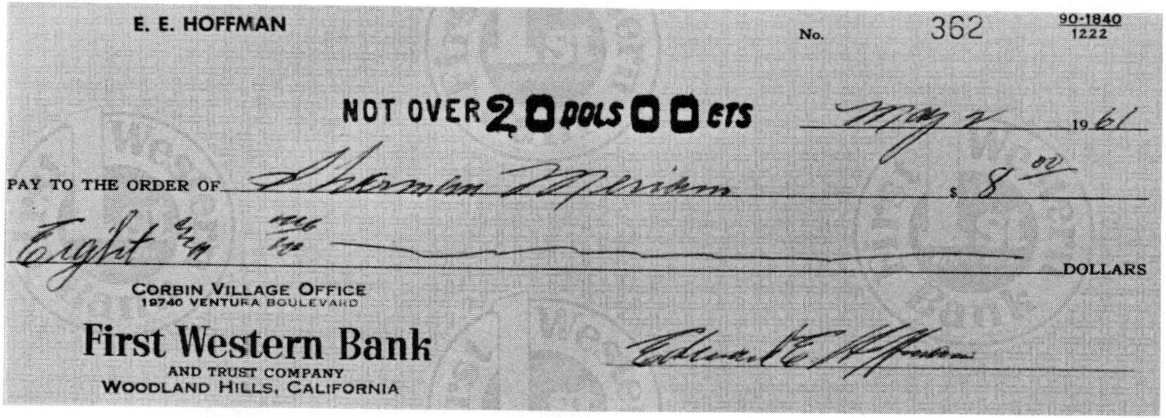

FIGURE 7

Although this check could easily be raised to $80.00, it would not be valid.

maximum value. You'll find the professional check artist will bypass your company. He won't be able to afford the time it takes to secure one of your signed checks. He's after the big game.

Many firms, rather than have the amount printed on the checks, will have a die made for their check protector that reads "not over" and the amount is then stamped in at the top of the check. However, before going to the expense of having such a die made, make sure that the protector you are using does not have a series of stars in front of the first figure, or a dollar sign. See the best type of imprint in Figure 7.

Although this particular check has been made out in long hand for $8.00 it could have very easily been changed to $80.00 had it not been stamped for a maximum value of $20.00.

Printing a maximum value on payroll checks is proving popular with more and more companies. This is done when checks are being printed and will show at bottom of check in printers' ink.

Once you sign a check, it's the only part of your business operation that you lose complete control of for a period of at least thirty days.

Any public speaker will tell you that you must start out with a statement that will be very interesting and command the audience's attention.

I have been able to do this with the following words when I talk to a service club where there may be *20 to 30 different types of businesses or professions represented.*

"I am ready to give $100.00 to your organization if any member here can name any part of his business that he loses complete control of for a period of 30 days.

"By that I mean: If you are a doctor and a patient has a relapse, you are notified immediately. If you are held up with a gun, you don't have to be told you are being held up. Should anyone break into your office or place of business, you are either notified by the police that night, or you find out about it when you open up in the morning. Should customers promise that they will be in on the 10th of the month to pay the money they owe you, if they haven't been in on the 11th, you know it.

"But when you send out or give someone a check on the 1st of the month, when do you see that check the next time?

Whether it be a $1.00 check or $10,000.00 check, you won't see it until the end of the month. And if it has not been deposited immediately, you will have difficulty locating it." Thirty days or longer can be a lifetime in the business world. Yet every day that check is out, your bank signature is out, too.

The routine is that the bank statement and your cancelled checks will arrive at the end of the month but there is another solution. If you have any doubt about the hands one of your checks has fallen into, you don't have to wait. Your bank will allow you to take a look at your checking account voucher whenever you make the request. By taking advantage of this service, you can know which checks are still outstanding and have not cleared your bank without waiting a full month.

If a check has not cleared your bank within a reasonable time, it's a good business practice to contact the person to whom it was made payable and find out why it hasn't been deposited. If there is any doubt in the payee's mind about where the check is, you can issue a Stop Payment Order on the check in question.

By utilizing the bank's services and looking at your checking account voucher, you will have some control over your outstanding checks.

OPENING THAT CHECKING ACCOUNT

WE LIVE IN a check-writing world. It's time to open that checking account if you're one of the few people left without one. Your bank is anxious for your business and is spending a great deal of money advertising and promoting the advantages of owning a checking account. In years gone by, to open a personal checking account, a bank required a prospective new customer to be introduced by a depositor in good standing. Today most banks are getting a little too eager. They vary as to how stringent their requirements are. In some cases, it's possible to open a new account with little or no identification, as long as you have a deposit ready to place into the account.

As part of my lecture program I have opened many, many checking accounts with absolutely no identification. Usually, I enter the bank clutching two $100.00 bills in my hand. I tell the manager I want to open a commercial checking account. He hands me two signature cards and watches me sign them. When he asks how much I want to deposit, I hand him the two $100.00 bills. When he asks for identification, I pretend to reach for my wallet. A look of anguish crosses my face as I tell him that I must have left my wallet in my room. I offer to return to get my wallet and mention I'll come back later in the day to open my account. Not wanting to lose the account, the manager decides he doesn't need the identification papers and asks for some banking references. Having used the name, William S. Borden, when opening accounts in other banks, I can always give a list of banks. The names of these banks are easy to recall because none of them required identification when I opened my account. The bank manager happily takes my two $100.00 bills and issues a passbook with an entry of $200.00. He then gives me a checkbook and tells me I can have my name imprinted on my checks at no extra charge. The reason I have usually been successful in obtaining a checking account, without presenting any identification, is a bank employee's over-eagerness not to lose a new account.

In most cases a bank is cautious, and if you're opening a new account this is the procedure you'll follow. The bank's first inquiry will be former bank references. With this information the bank will send a signature card requesting verification of your signature. You will be asked routine questions as to where you're employed, how long you've lived in the city, and your present address. Don't be annoyed with the question. Be glad you're dealing with a cautious bank. This is the bank you're planning to entrust with your money. You'll then be asked to show as much identification as you have. Usually your service discharge papers, a driver's license, employment card, union membership card are all good means of identification. They will be enough to satisfy the bank executive interviewing you.

You will be given several signature cards and asked to sign each one. If you feel this is a bother, remember your signature is the key that unlocks the door to the money the bank will be holding for you. Your signature will be compared with that on the identification papers you have shown. Another reason you must sign more than one signature card is that various departments of the bank handling your account will need access to a signature card.

What did the last signature card you signed really say?

If you don't remember what it said, the next time you visit your bank ask to see a copy of a signature card. Almost no one bothers to read this card. The concentration is on the blank line you're signing. The card states you must abide by the rules and regulations of the bank. If you had taken the time to read this agreement and balked at signing it, your new account would not be accepted by the bank. But since you, like every other new depositor, didn't stop to read what you were signing, let's move to the next operation in opening a new checking account.

Now you'll be asked how much money you want to deposit in your new account. The minimum allowed varies with the type of checking account you're opening.

A special checking account can be opened with a very small amount of money as the bank charges you a service fee for the checks you use, plus a monthly service charge.

A regular checking account will require a minimum balance, usually amounting to $500.00. By maintaining this minimum balance you are not required to pay a service charge. This minimum balance varies with the bank and in one case runs as high as $5,000.00. You will be given a receipt for the money or check you are depositing. The next discussion will be the style of check you will use and whether or not you want your name imprinted on your checks. In most cases your check book will be mailed to you, particularly if you're having your name imprinted. (See the next chapter which covers the pros and cons of imprinting checks.) In some cases you'll be given a pass book, but most banks use duplicate deposit slips instead. In larger banks, you will be assigned a coded account number. You'll learn more about this new step toward mechanization in our banks in You're Now a Number (Page 67).

If this happens to be your first checking account, there are a few simple rules to remember to protect yourself and your bank balance.

A single check with your recognizable signature is worth all the money you have in your checking account. Don't be careless with your checkbook or your signature. You wouldn't leave your wallet or pocketbook containing all the money you owned exposed for strangers to help themselves.

So make sure, when you're making out a check, that you don't expose the stub with your bank balance for the casual observance of strangers. People are naturally curious and will take a look if you allow it. Some of them mean no harm, but this is one way that confidence men and check artists find out if your bank balance is worth the effort.

In opening a business or company checking account, you will be required to have all persons who are authorized to sign checks sign signature cards. In some states in which you are operating under a trade name, you will be required to bring in proof that you are legitimately in business under that name. Proof can be in the form of a business license and/or newspaper advertisement displaying the trade name.

The bank will also require a copy of the by-laws of the company. This usually includes a section devoted to the signing of the company's checks, the names and positions of the officers of the company, and their terms of office. You will be questioned about the type of company you're starting, its business address, its products, and other details. A discussion will follow concerning the type of check books that will best serve your company's needs and whether the bank will furnish same or the company will have its own printed.

Finally you will be given a printed set of rules and regulations governing the company's association with the bank. Be sure to read these rules and regulations and ask questions if there are any points that puzzle you.

THE IMPRINTED CHECK

WHEN YOU open a checking account, the bank will submit samples of checks for your approval. If it's a personal account, you usually have a choice of two types of check books, either the flat style or the style that folds over, similar to a billfold.

With a personal account, you're given a choice of whether or not your name will be imprinted on the checks. Since on a personal account there is no charge for the imprinting, most customers decide in favor of this free service. There is a fee for imprinting company checks. Most people like the feeling of seeing their names imprinted on their checks. Whether they admit it or not, it makes them feel more important.

The main advantage of imprinted checks is the value to the person or company to whom the check is made payable. How many times have you studied a signature on a check trying to figure out who wrote it? Also, it seems to be easier to cash a check with a name imprinted on it. Whether he'll admit it or not, the average businessman is more impressed with a customer's check if the customer's name is imprinted on the check. One forgery ring took advantage of the businessman's respect for the imprinted check by imprinting the names of seven companies on phony checks and successfully cashed them.

The only disadvantage of an imprinted check is that it does reveal information about you and, as a result, about your bank account. There is an easy and simple solution but most people neglect to use it.

If you decide in favor of imprinting your name on your checks, _don't have your full bank signature imprinted_. If your full bank signature reads Edward E. Hoffman, then your checks should be imprinted E. E. Hoffman. See Figure 8. Be sure to call this difference to the attention of your bank. Should your checkbook be lost or stolen and the finder has larceny in his heart, he'd sign the check E. E. Hoffman which would be the only information he'd have. He'd also spend considerable time trying to locate a copy of this particular signature.

When a bank pays out your funds on a signature that is spelled incorrectly or incompletely, _the burden of proof is on the bank_ and not the depositor, whereas, if you have your signature printed in the same manner as you use signing the check, if the forgery is even a fair forgery, _the burden of proof is on you_. Then it is that you are required to fill out time consuming reports and have them notarized. If the bank should honor the E. E. Hoffman signature, it would certainly be held liable. You would not even be required to fill out affidavits and notarizations which you would have to do if the forgery was a reasonable facsimile of your banking signature. The bank would readily admit its responsibility. Under customary circumstances the bank would have automatically rejected the forger's check signed E. E. Hoffman and returned it with the notation, "Irregular Signature."

Anyone can make a mistake, whether he be a banker or a customer. But here's a case where you'll be in trouble if you fail to notify the bank _you've_ made a mistake. Let's suppose you're the same customer by the name of Edward E. Hoffman. This is the bank signature you use. Suppose through carelessness, you should sign a check E. E. Hoffman and fail

FIGURE 8

A good form of protection; the signature differs from the imprinted name.

55

to call it to your bank's attention. If the bank should honor the check, or any others using this signature, the bank would be absolved of liability should there ever be a claim. It was *your* responsibility to call this error to the attention of your bank.

When you have business checks imprinted, be sure to have the firm's name, telephone number and address imprinted.

Make it simple for a merchant who is about to cash a check, drawn on your account, to reach you if he notices anything suspicious about it.

Be sure that the name of the person who signs your firm's checks is imprinted differently than his banking signature.

The reasons for doing this with your personal account are doubly important to your business account.

Millions of dollars in checks have been cashed by stores all over the country because of a local firm's name on the check. They had been stolen from a contractor's office, store or machine shop. People do not realize that their check book is one of the most valuable assets they have in their place of business. Recently a thief was caught selling 600 blank checks with a very well known firm name imprinted to a check passers ring for $3500.000. The total original cost to the firm from which the checks were stolen was $5.90.

Now, say you were running a retail business and some nice man came in to cash a check that he supposedly received from the plant down the street. He seemed to fit the payee name, and furnished convincing identification. Later you find out that the secretary left the check book out all night. Someone broke in and took the checks. He started passing them throughout the neighborhood. You would have paid out hard-earned money and merchandise, because of someone's negligence.

The businessman who is careless with his check book is certainly no help to his community or his neighbors. By keeping your blank checks locked up or at least out of sight, you will be doing everybody a favor.

If your company goes out of business or changes its name, don't put the left-over imprinted blank checks in boxes and forget about them. There is only one thing to do with blank checks that have no purpose in your business, destroy them. By destroying them, I do not mean putting them in cardboard boxes for the trash man to collect. I mean only one thing, *burn the checks*. This is the *only* way you can be assured that these checks will not return to haunt you and your bank.

If you decide not to have your name or names printed on your personal checks, it is advisable to have the bank imprint them with numbers only. Remember, your magnetic account number is at the bottom of the check, and this is what the banks go by, not name. You would have better control and also know whether any check numbers are missing or stolen. It is also more difficult to try altering a printed number as opposed to one written in by hand.

I'VE PROVEN time and time again that it is possible to make erasures and changes on checks using "safety paper" and still have the checks cashed at the bank. But "safety paper" has stopped many amateurs from trying to cash checks they were trying to alter, and has at least slowed down the professional check artist. So, by all means, use "safety paper."

Today your bank and the printers who manufacture and print checks for personal accounts and business firms generally use a white bond paper coated with aniline dye. Aniline dye is very sensitive ink that rubs off when erased, whether the check is typed, written with pen, or with the softest lead pencil. When erased, the check reveals the white stock of the bond paper underneath. A check bearing this warning sign should make any cashier or businessman suspicious.

If the bank has a check that it has any doubt about, yet feels the erasure on a check is legitimate, in most cases the maker will be contacted and asked to come into the bank and initial the erasure. This, of course, is all the protection the bank needs.

As a businessman if you have any doubt about a possible erasure on a check, don't cash it. If it happens to be a very good customer's check and it's his personal check, ask him to write out another check or have him sign his full bank signature next to the erasure. Although the bank accepts initials, the businessman should ask for a full signature.

Standard "safety paper" can be purchased in any stationery store. You'll find this paper uses a single sensitive ink coating with a design made up of straight lines. Some banks use a single coated "safety paper" made expressly for their use and it contains the banks' own specific designs. Known as the Lithographic Pantograph System, this "safety paper" uses a lithograph press and applies a sensitive ink, creating a design in the background tint. Some other banks have a popular "safety paper" known as the Wet Process. A plain white bond is covered with fugitive or sensitive ink wavy lines and a subsequent safety tint, which is sensitive to most chemical alterations.

Before the popularity of "safety paper", ink eradicator was often used by the criminal in changing checks. But he soon learned that, when this bleaching agent makes contact with "safety paper", that spot on the check turns white. Ink eradicator is not successful in removing anything written with a Prussian blue ball point pen. However, this can be overcome and I'll explain how in a later chapter. (See Altered Checks.)

There is a "safety paper" that has an amazing selling appeal. The salesman holds the check up to a strong light, pointing out that it looks like any other check. Then he applies ink eradicator to the check's safety ink coating and, as if by magic, small printed words . . . "void" appear on the check wherever the eradicator made contact on the paper. This sales feature makes quite an impression on the prospective buyer and he's positive he's found the perfect check protection.

Figure 9 shows a check issued for $200.00. Note the printed decimal point in the "net check" space. This forces the writer to start too far away from the $ sign making it

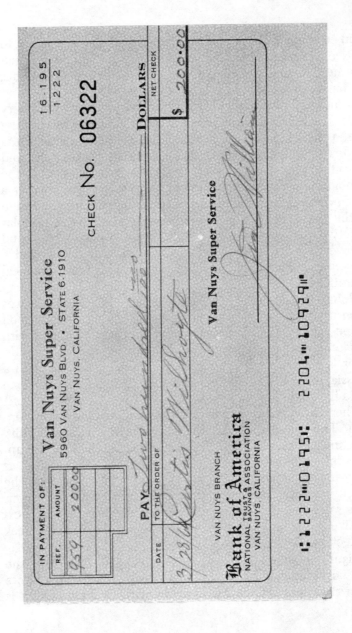

60

Figure 9

Before: This check looks like ordinary safety paper.

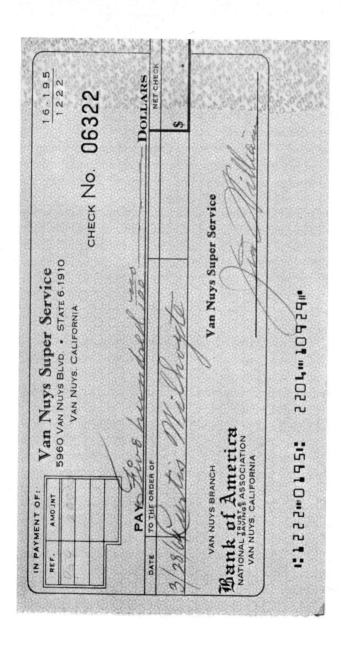

FIGURE 10

After: Removing the amount from the payment box and making an alteration with a pen did not bring out the word "Void."

61

unsafe. Figure 10 shows the same check treated with two different chemicals. One, a commercial ink eradicator, that when applied, did as they claimed, brought out the word "VOID". The second, removed writing from the "in payment of box" without showing the word "VOID". I have had many calls for formula two.

I've discovered it's easier in some cases to make an erasure on this type of paper. Such erasures are less noticeable than those made on regularly coated "safety paper". However, no pro will use eradicator on any check.

Printing companies specializing in "safety paper" use even more precautionary methods than I've mentioned so far. Some give as many as three or more safety coatings. A good grade of white bond is treated with acid or iodine, followed by a lithographing with sensitive ink patterns, and finally a lathework border using regular ink. The result is a three-layer protection for the check. Any "safety paper" containing iodine will turn a brownish red and eventually will turn white when ink eradicator comes in contact with it.

Printers will develop any type of design you request. All wavy line patterns, triangles, etc., utilizing sensitive inks are patented by the manufacturers and their originality and indi-viduality are respected by one another.

You'll find the good printer will be working to protect you and guard your checks. Recently a large forgery ring was apprehended because the ring had purchased many reams of "safety paper" and ordered them shipped immediately to a nearby city. The individual placing the order decided he did not want the checks imprinted with his company's name. The customer was a new one and paid cash. The printer had no reason not to accept the order and shipped the "safety paper" to the nearby city. Nevertheless, questions began to plague the printer and he couldn't come up with the answers. He couldn't understand why a company needing so much "safety paper" would not want its company name imprinted on the checks. Also, why hadn't the customer purchased the "safety paper" in his own city? This seemed strange particularly since the customer seemed to be in such a rush for the order.

He finally came to a wise decision and put in a call to the sheriff's office in the nearby city. He informed the sheriff of a large order of "safety paper" he had shipped to a new customer to an address and company located in the sheriff's city. Unable to find any record of a legitimate business at the address the printer had given him, the sheriff started an investigation. At the customer's address the sheriff and his men discovered hundreds of "safety checks" imprinted with the names of well-known local firms.

The forging material confiscated by the sheriff included a portable printing press, trays of dies, quantities of printers' ink and license plates. This forging ring's scheme to rob local firms of thousands and thousands of dollars was stopped before it was able to cash its first phony check. The entire community owed a vote of thanks to an alert printer in another city who was aware of the danger of letting "safety paper" fall into the wrong hands.

Now the question comes to your mind . . . "Is 'safety paper' really safe?" The various coatings used on "safety paper" protect you from the amateur. The first time he is tempted to apply ink eradicator or an eraser to a "safety paper" check and finds a white spot staring up at him, the temptation may leave him and he may get back on the "honest track."

It's a different matter with the professional check artist. He knows the tricks of his trade and he also is aware of the manufacturers' protective measures. The U. S. Post Office Department sent out a bulletin which covered the upswing in the forgery crime wave and warned about chemicals on the market that will remove pigmentation from some types of ink without turning the "safety paper" white.

FIGURE 11

AFTER: If you <u>had</u> this check, would your bank accept this for deposit?

64

FIGURE 12

Before: This check has not been treated with chemicals.

A good example of how this chemical works is shown in Figures 11 and 12. Note that the check did not turn white nor was it damaged in any way. This makes it possible to <u>fill in any payee name</u>, or change to a larger amount.

If the professional check artist does happen to turn the "safety paper" white or removes the design on the paper, he knows how to restore the paper after altering the check to suit his needs. This is a tedious and time-consuming operation and can be successfully accomplished only on the cheapest paper. The check artist has the time and the patience if your bank balance is large enough to make the effort worth while. He can fill perforations, remove printing and lithographic ink, and then restore the physical elements of the check.

But his greatest aid is *not* his skill, but the *businessman's carelessness* with his checks and his signature.

An important legal decision rendered by the United States Supreme Court in the case of the Leather Manufacturers versus Morgan, 171 U.S. 96, should wake you up to the importance of protecting your check book with the same care as you use in handling cash.

"The maker of check is obliged to use all due diligence in protecting it; the omission to use the most effectual protection against alteration, is evidence of neglect, which renders him responsible for the fraudulent amount, the bank being responsible only for the apparent genuineness of the signature and ordinary care in paying a check."

Protecting your bank balance not only is a *good idea,* but it's your *legal responsibility.*

The forger, whether professional or amateur, has one partner who gives banks and law enforcement agencies the most trouble and he is the careless check writer! Don't make your bank balance an easy target. Start off on the right foot by making the forger's job a little more difficult by writing your checks on "safety paper" that is well protected.

YOU'RE NOW A NUMBER

IT WON'T BE long until you'll walk into your bank and be greeted by a bank clerk with "Good morning, 027-234." She'll be talking to you. Along with being known as a number of the new coding system and the introduction of automation in all banks, the customer will find more and more responsibility falling on his shoulders.

There was a time when banks gave a gold watch to an employee for serving twenty-five years. But each year banks are reporting a yearly loss of better than 45% of their employees. With this alarming turnover, bank officials and electronic engineers have put their heads together to find the new twenty-five year man. The "man" they've come up with is four feet high, four feet wide, and twenty feet long. If he completes his twenty-five years, I wonder what his gold watch will look like?

This "man" the wizards have come up with really is a check-sorting machine that can process 750 to 1,500 checks per minute. The average worker was able to process only ten checks per minute. This mechanical device has replaced quite a few workers, cut down the handling time on checks, and removed one of the big headaches of trying to decipher signatures that are sometimes illegible. The magnetic ink automatically picked the right account by number. Of course, there are mistakes. Banks feel the time and money the machine saves is worth any minor problems. One sorting office can handle checks from as many as 20 branch banks. And who has seen a machine take a coffee break, ask for more money, or even look for a better job? It seems the bank managers are happy with their new employees. But what about the customers? That's the problem. The customer's check is now an added responsibility. The customer must keep a wary eye on his blank checks which contain magnetic ink characters. With the new automation it would be possible for a check to slip through without having a signature that vaguely resembled the customer's bank signature. An unhappy memory in the mind of our electronic wizards is the case in which a very nice gray-haired man opened a checking account in a bank which used a coding system. Everything seemed to be in order and the new customer asked for a commercial check book which contains three checks to a page. When the gray-haired man received the checks, the clerk pointed out that his account number was printed on the check in magnetic ink and that he would also find deposit slips in the back of his check book.

The clerk also pointed out that the customer would find his account number printed in magnetic ink on the deposit slips, too. The gray-haired man told the clerk that he approved of progress and he always tried to keep up with the times. Here was one gray-haired man who did keep up with the times, and, I might add, the bank's automation. He took some of the deposit slips from the back of his check book and placed them neatly on the various counters in the bank lobby. These were the deposit slips that contained *his* account number in magnetic ink. Each day he would return and pick up any unused deposit slips bearing his account number. Are you wondering what he was doing? Other customers hurried into the bank, picked up the gray-haired man's deposit slips, filled out their deposits, and left their money with the bank. The money was neither safe, nor was it sound. When these deposit slips were processed, even though the depositors wrote their name and address on the deposit slips, the machine credited the total deposit to the account number which belonged to this man, who had quite a few thousand to his credit, although the only deposit he had made was for $100.00.

The gray-haired man really did keep up with the times and gave the automation wizards a real problem.

In this case the bank was liable.

With a machine sorting by use of magnetic numbers, it is possible for this kind of freak case to occur. The automation boys would rather forget all about it. In the future, make sure you are using your own deposit slips, or at least blank ones furnished by the bank. Check the slip to make sure that your account number is on it and you're safe.

The bank's automation has brought another responsibility to the customer. You may not have thought of yourself as a number to your bank, but lend one of your own checks to a friend and see what could happen. Suppose a friend by the name of Bixby owes you twenty dollars and wants to pay you. It happens he doesn't have the cash or a blank check. Mr. Bixby borrows one of your personal checks, fills it out for twenty dollars, and signs it. At the end of the month when your bank statement arrives, you discover Mr. Bixby's twenty-dollar check was charged to your account. You notify Mr. Bixby, who promises to get the twenty dollars to you soon. When you notify the bank of its error, you are informed that the charge was an oversight. More important, you are given a lecture on never lending a coded check to anyone. Machines may be mechanical brains, but they haven't replaced the alert, thinking individual. If automation continues, more and more responsibility will become the customer's.

You may be known as "John Smith" among your friends; at your bank you'll be known by digits. Keep smiling; the bank manager is.

IDENTIFY THAT STRANGER!

IF A STRANGER comes into your place of business and wants a check cashed, you're better off if you can have him identified by someone you know and trust. If he can't furnish this kind of identification and instead offers a person who is also unknown to you, don't follow his suggestion. The unknown person could be his accomplice who will be more than willing to supply you with all the *mis*information you want.

The businessman who accepts checks must train himself as to what identification is acceptable. When you ask for identification, see what the stranger offers you—don't be specific about what you expect.

ACCEPTABLE IDENTIFICATION includes the following:

Driver's license—Make sure the description fits the person. Compare signature on license with handwriting on check. Compare serial number in upper right hand corner with previous license in lower left hand corner. Feel more secure if the numbers are the same.

Temporary Renewal Permit—Examine as you would a permanent license, especially the serial numbers.

Employment Card—This is a good identification if it bears a picture and signature. Examine carefully.

Charge-a-plates—These can be used as identification if augmented with a handwriting sample.

Credit Cards—Make sure they have not expired.

If the passer is a man, ask him his birth date. Find out general area where he lives, where he works and type of work he performs. See if this agrees with his general appearance. Use the same technique with a woman but you may have to skip the question about her birth date.

POOR IDENTIFICATION—Accept none of the following, if presented alone:

Social Security Card
Bank Pass Book
Voter's Registration
Library Card
Gasoline Credit Card
Employment Badge—if it contains only a number.
Temporary Driver's License—If this is the only identification, it often spells a bad check.

If the passer gives you something containing his handwriting for comparison, different combinations of the poor identifications may be acceptable. But use your judgement.

Any identification that is accepted, should be noted on the back of the check.

You will never find another customer as impatient for the cash he's trying to get as the bad check artist. If you have any doubt about the customer's check, just slow down a bit.

The smartest move you can make is to mention you're going to call the bank, or the firm on which the check is drawn. Go to the phone and pretend to make the call, even if you know the bank has been closed for hours and everybody's gone home. You'll be surprised how often, if your suspicions are accurate, your customer will be gone when you return from the phone. You'll be holding a bad check that didn't cost you a penny.

If you feel these precautions are too tough on your customers, remember they are not aimed at your reliable good customers. The target is the talkative stranger who insists upon cashing a check.

YOUR ENDORSEMENT—A RESPONSIBILITY

Do YOU KNOW what your obligation is when you add your name to the back of a check that already has a string of endorsements? If you don't, this news may come as quite a shock.

Unless you qualify your endorsement as to the obligations you're willing to undertake, your endorsement guarantees that you have good title to the check and all the endorsers listed above your endorsement had good title. Your endorsement also states the check is valid at the time of your endorsement.

Now what does all this mean?

It means endorsers are liable in the order in which they have endorsed the check. When the final holder of the check presents it to the bank and is refused payment, he must notify the original drawer of the check and the endorsers immediately. He will try to recover his loss from the drawer or the person from whom he received the check. But the responsibility could end up *yours alone*, particularly if you had signed your name as an endorser below another endorsement that proved to be a forgery.

Make sure all endorsers put their full address below their names so they can be easily contacted in case of a problem.

Now let's take a check made payable to you. Once you have endorsed this type of check, you are no longer holding a piece of paper, you are holding cash. If you're planning to deposit it to your bank account personally, you should wait and endorse it at the bank. If you're mailing the check to the bank or sending it by any one else, make sure that you make the notation "For deposit only" above your endorsement.

If for any reason you find it necessary to mail or send by messenger a check made payable to you to a third party, perhaps a "J. J. Smith" as payment for some obligation, on the back of the check you should endorse it, "Pay to the order of 'J. J. Smith'" with your endorsement underneath.

A blank endorsement (meaning just your endorsement) would allow anyone to cash if it happened to get lost on its way to Mr. Smith. By endorsing the check with the special endorsement, the check requires "J. J. Smith's" signature in order to be cashed.

A good rule to remember when endorsing any checks received by you is to be sure to *endorse it exactly as the check is drawn.*

If it's made payable to "Raymond L. King," it should be endorsed "Raymond L. King" and not "R. L. King."

If your name or your firm's name is misspelled, endorse it with the incorrect spelling and then sign the correct name underneath.

A man was informed by an attorney that he would have to support his girl friends baby due in 3 months. The man explained to the attorney he had spent the past 2 years in jail and had only known this girl 3 months. Why should he be responsible? The attorney informed him that according to the law, "When you cannot locate the original maker, the last endorser is always liable".

ALL THE ADVICE I've given in my chapter "Identify That Stranger!" applies to any endorser unknown to you. Can you afford to lose $5,000.00? No one can. But I have a case where a businessman did. You, too, could be a victim unless you're ready to start following a new golden rule . . . *Know your endorser.* This case may get you on the right track.

John Smith was indebted to Paul Brown to the extent of $5,000. Smith gave Brown a $5,000 check. Brown made a deal with an accomplice to forge his endorsement on the back of the check. From here on out in this case I'll refer to the accomplice as Brown-B and the real Paul Brown as Brown-A.

The accomplice impersonating Paul Brown (Brown-B) took the check into a wholesale house stating that he wished to make a purchase. The wholesale house was given the $5,000 check. Brown-B told the manager of the wholesale house to deposit the check and when it cleared the out-of-state bank on which it was drawn, Brown-B would pick up the merchandise he wanted and the balance in cash.

After waiting three days the accomplice, Brown-B had the wholesale house manager wire the out-of-state bank to confirm his check's clearance. The bank confirmed by wire that the check was good and the signature valid. The check had been honored.

Brown-B then obtained $1,000 in merchandise and a check drawn by the wholesaler for $4,000. Brown-B cashed the wholesaler's check and reported his success to the original Paul Brown. The accomplice took his cut of the profits and left town for parts unknown.

As the case goes so far you'd think Paul Brown had lost his mind, but you'll soon see the method to his madness. Paul Brown called John Smith, the writer of the $5,000 check, and informed Mr. Smith that he had lost the check or it had been stolen. He asked John Smith to issue a Stop Payment Order on the check.

John Smith wired his bank issuing the Stop Payment Order. By return wire the bank notified him that the check had already been honored. John Smith was forced to issue another check to Paul Brown.

The forged endorsement was charged back to the wholesaler costing him a total of $4,000 in cash and $1,000 in merchandise. This wholesaler learned an expensive lesson in KNOWING YOUR ENDORSER.

This type of operation could be worked on any business today and works even better when smaller amounts are involved.

The check should always be endorsed in your presence. If it's already endorsed, have the party endorse it again at the opposite end of the check. Any check made payable to two or more persons must be correctly endorsed by all parties and they must all endorse the check in your presence. If the check has other endorsements, make sure you have the addresses of all the endorsers. The bank will return any check that is improperly endorsed. Make sure the payee's name and endorsement agree. Above all follow my advice on identifying strangers and you won't go wrong if you know your endorser!

POSTAL THIEVES

THE UNITED STATES Post Office handles more money in the form of checks than the largest bank chain in the world. It is understandable that in the last eight years arrests for thefts of mail outside post offices have increased 192%. Through the use and display of posters such as shown in Figure 16, the FBI and Postal Inspectors seek the aid of all citizens in apprehending such criminals.

Organized gangs are moving from city to city intercepting mail. These gangs are not after the package your wife may be sending for your aunt's birthday. These gangs are after checks and money and they prey on every spot where mail is assembled. It may be a spot as simple as your office mail basket for outgoing mail, and it runs to robbing mail boxes and stealing loaded mail sacks.

Sometimes the gangs sell the checks to a fence who has his own ways of turning them into cash. Naturally, the fence pays a low rate for the checks that may be raised and cashed for much larger sums than the original figures. For the gangs that handle the raising and cashing of checks personally, these checks turn into fantastic income. That's the reason the gangs often handle the operation from beginning to end, or until they're caught.

FIGURE 13

Fold check over in *middle of signature*, so that it cannot be traced by holding a light behind the envelope.

The penalties when these thieves are caught vary with the judge trying the case. In an Eastern city a short time ago a local police officer caught a postal thief running down a railroad right-of-way with a mail sack under his arm. He was booked on suspicion of robbing the mails. Federal agents were notified, but prosecution was declined in favor of local authorities. The local judge fined the thief $25.00. The postal thief paid the fine and was released.

With cases like this being repeated throughout the United States, the criminal is going to come out with a new slogan, "CRIME *DOES* PAY!" Judges in our Federal Courts measure out sterner sentences the maximum being five years in prison or a $2,000.00 fine, or both, for each offense.

The check you send through the mails bears your authentic signature and, as you've been reminded before, the key to your bank account. This is the reason why banks report more and more bank statements and cancelled checks are missing in the mails.

From the moment a check you've signed leaves your desk to the moment it arrives back on your desk as a cancelled check can be anywhere from thirty days to sixty days. During this time you have no control over this valuable piece of paper. Many people handle your check from the moment it leaves your desk.

It's important that you learn how to mail a check. If you do not fold your check properly and use a regular long envelope that is unlined, any one of the people who handles your envelope can hold it up to a light and trace your valuable signature on another piece of paper. Figure 13 shows a check folded in an envelope the *wrong* way, as the signature is completely exposed. Folding over *half* of the signature makes it *impossible* to retrace.

Strangely enough, most businessmen feel the necessity for hiding and camouflaging the *amount* of the check. The *im-*

portant part of your check is the recognizable signature upon which the bank will cash checks.

Popular crime and detective television shows have long ago revealed one of the trade secrets of postal thieves. In case you missed the shows that opened the use of this old device to new potential thieves, here's how you can remove a check from a sealed envelope without steaming it open.

You use two knitting needles that have been welded together at the broad end. Into the breather space of the sealed flap of the envelope insert the pointed ends of the needles with one needle under the check and the other over the check. Then by rolling the needles, the check is wrapped around the needle and is easily slipped out of the envelope through the breather space. See Figure 14. *You can beat the thieves* at their own game by folding a check or currency so that the ends of the check reach from one end of the envelope to the other. When the check is placed in the envelope in this manner, it's impossible to straddle it. See Figure 17 which shows the correct way of placing a check in an envelope.

Now I've spent some time telling you about postal thieves and gangs. I don't want you to get the impression that these gangs have taken over your post office. Far from it. The U.S. Postal Inspectors represent the oldest law enforcement agency in the United States. Last year they made 8,898 arrests for violations of Federal postal laws. Conviction for such crimes equalled almost 100%. If a check you've mailed should get lost in the mails, these are the men who will have the headache of trying to find it for you.

The Post Office, like most of our banks, works on the principle that most people are honest. In dealing with billions of dollars in valuables each year, the postal inspectors are there to protect you.

With over half a million people employed by the Post Office throughout the country, temptation will naturally overcome a few people. The Post Office has installed an ob-

FIGURE 14

A simple way to remove check from envelope without opening it.

Post Office Department
OFFICE OF THE INSPECTOR-IN-CHARGE

W. E. Cochran
Inspector in Charge

WARNING

TO ALL BANKS AND TRUST COMPANIES

THIS DEPARTMENT HAS RECEIVED NUMEROUS COMPLAINTS OF THE LOSS OF LETTERS CONTAINING CHECKS.

Many of these checks have been altered by changing the date, by removing the name of the payee with chemicals and inserting the word "BEARER," and if the amount of the check is small this is removed and a higher amount, usually $200.00 or more, inserted. The alterations in the check are made so cleverly that the most minute examination will not disclose any erasures.

The altered check is then taken to the bank on which it is drawn, usually a bank within a radius of 100 miles of cities, and is presented. In most cases the paying teller pays over the money without question, because he recognizes the signature of the maker of the check.

This office is interested in the matter on account of the theft of mail matter from hall letter boxes. For the detection of the persons responsible for these thefts and the forgery of the checks, we must have the assistance of the banks, and unless the persons interested desire to prosecute for forgery in the State Courts the offenders will be prosecuted in the U. S. Courts for theft of mail. Or they might possibly be prosecuted on both charges.

It is therefore, requested that all bank employes carefully scrutinize all 'BEARER' and 'CASH' checks presented at the bank, and, if the person presenting the same is not known, that the maker of the check be communicated with at once, before payment.

It has been learned that, if the paying teller makes any move to go to the telephone, the forger presenting the check will immediately leave the bank, without the check. In this correction the bank employees can render an important service by endeavoring to apprehend the forger with the aid of local officers.

The banks in the vicinity have been defrauded of thousands of dollars in the manner above described, and it is confidently expected that they will co-operate in the matter of apprehending the forger.

It is requested that the undersigned be notified at once in the event of arrest in such a case, by telephone, or telegraph, Goverment rate, collect.

W. E. COCHRAN
Post Office Inspector in Charge

FIGURE 15

PLEASE POST

CASE NO. 98582-K
126404-MD
Dec. 14, 1960

POST OFFICE DEPARTMENT
INSPECTION SERVICE
Office of the Inspector in Charge
SAN FRANCISCO 1, CALIFORNIA

Fingerprint Classification
9 0 17 Wr 14   19 Dr 19 14
— L 19 Wr —   19 Dd 19 15

FBI NO. 397 262 D

WANTED WANTED

ALTERING, FORGING, AND UTTERING
U. S. POSTAL MONEY ORDERS

MICHAEL SEDON

Aliases: William Lowman, Sr.
Louis Hart

DESCRIPTION: Born 6/24/26 Penn.; 6 ft. 1 in.,
210, brown eyes, black hair, hairless mole right cheek
near earlobe, soft spoken. Russian-Polish extraction.

MICHAEL SEDON   FBI #397 262 D

Signature of person fingerprinted

(Handwriting and fingerprints on reverse).

U. S. MARSHAL, LOS ANGELES, CALIF. HOLDS COMMISSIONER WARRANT CHARGING MICHAEL SEDON WITH ALTERING AND FORGING POSTAL MONEY ORDER AT LOS ANGELES ON APRIL 5, 1960. BAIL $5,000.00. SEDON ALSO SUBJECT OF PAROLE VIOLATION WARRANT HELD BY U. S. MARSHAL, SEATTLE, WASH.

SEDON has record forgery conviction 1959 in B. C. Canada and Dyer Act 1/14/60, Seattle, Wash., and placed on probation. In March 1960, he was employed by loan firm, Seattle, and absconded with postal money orders payable to firm, a Sheraton Hotel credit card and other credentials of William H. Lowman, official of firm. Money orders altered to show payable to Michael Sedon or William Lowman and cashed Tacoma, Wash. and Los Angeles.

From May to Oct. 30, 1960, SEDON was employed as cafe counterman at Amboy, Calif., as LOUIS HART. He stole from Amboy post office adjacent to cafe blank money orders Nos. 12-87,989,900 through 12-87,990,000.

In Nov. 1960, SEDON passed two stolen money orders at Las Vegas, Nev. and 22 at Chicago, Ill. for $100 each showing payee name as William Lowman in all but one instance when payee was shown as A. Pulos.

SEDON still in possession remaining 76 money orders which he may attempt to cash. Any name, date, or amount to $100, or post office name may be shown, but they are identifiable by the above numbers.

IF SEDON IS LOCATED, CAUSE IMMEDIATE ARREST AND NOTIFY NEAREST POSTAL INSPECTOR OR THE UNDERSIGNED BY TELEPHONE OR TELETYPE COLLECT.

POSTAL INSPECTORS
LOS ANGELES 53, CALIF.
Telephone: MA 5-7411, Ext. 677
Teletype: LA 118

POSTAL INSPECTOR IN CHARGE
SAN FRANCISCO 1, CALIF.
Telephone: MA 1-2500, Ext. 2340
Teletype: SF 424

GPO WLNS

FIGURE 16

The Post Office Department solicits the aid of all citizens in apprehending wanted criminals with posters such as this in Post Offices.

servation system to protect your property and to discourage the few people that may be tempted. The observation system consists of a one-way mirror placed at the top of the wall of the post office, similar to what some markets are using for spotting shoplifters. Behind it is a corridor for a postal inspector to observe the activities going on within the post office. When the U. S. Postal Inspectors receive a report that thefts are taking place in a particular post office or district, a postal inspector is assigned to this trouble spot and he uses the observation system to watch out for any unusual activity. None of the employees knows when a postal inspector is observing. Some employees have objected to the use of this system to watch them. It has kept many honest employees from making that one fatal mistake and it has discouraged professional thieves from seeking employment with the Post Office.

FIGURE 17

If check fills envelope from end to end, it cannot be removed without tearing.

THE CHECK ARTIST GOES RURAL

MANY OF OUR larger ranches and farms are run as large companies and have offices from which they operate. All the advice I've given for the operation of a successful business in a city applies to the large ranches and farms.

But today we still have many small farms and ranches which are run as a one-man operation most of the year, with hired hands added when needed. These farmers and ranchers do not have an office, instead they transact most of their business out of their hip pockets. They handle most of their business by check, not only paying their debts by check, but being compensated almost entirely by check. In the course of one business day a farmer or rancher carries around a number of checks received from customers. These checks may be found sticking out of his pockets, in his billfold, or even more likely in his checkbook which is probably lying on the seat of his pickup truck or car. This manner of conducting business is what has brought the check artist to the farm and ranch. You can be assured the check artist is neither interested in horses and chickens, nor is he interested in raising alfalfa and corn. What he is interested in is getting his hands on the farmer's checks and checkbook.

The product the check artist wants to raise is the farmer's check. As long as the farmer continues this easy-going bookkeeping system, he's going to be a target for the professional check artist.

Don't expect to be able to recognize the check artist by his city ways and business suit. He probably will show up in a rented pickup truck, a pair of bluejeans and a denim shirt. His accent will match yours and he'll have a whole new personality that will come in handy to confuse and distract cashiers and businessmen when he cashes your stolen checks after raising them to larger sums with a few careful strokes of his pen. Ranchers should be careful when hiring migratory workers seeking "one day's employment." Their checks are usually for small sums and ranchers are apt to be a little careless in writing them. Particularly vulnerable are checks in the amounts of 6, 8 or 10 dollars which can easily be raised to 60, 80 or 70 dollars. The check artist will be on the look-out for "one day" jobs and "one day" checks.

The farmer will often excuse his carelessness with his checks and checkbook by telling you that often many of his workers cannot speak the English language, much less write it. The farmer feels if they can't write out good checks, his workers couldn't possible write out bad checks. One fact he forgets is there is a big market for blank checks. A smart check artist will pay cash dollars for the farmer's blank checks.

One farmer learned an expensive lesson when he gave a free hand to a contractor who furnished migratory workers to bring in his crop. At the end of the season the farmer wrote out checks for the workers and gave them to the contractor who had been more than helpful during the season. The farmer felt lucky having such a devoted man in charge of the workers. The contractor kept the good checks and gave the workers checks he had forged, using blank checks he had stolen from the back of the farmer's checkbook. The contractor instructed the workers to cash the checks in the local stores rather than the bank because it would be another day before the farmer would deposit the full amount of money in the bank to cover the checks. He then endorsed all the workers' good checks himself and the farmer drove him to the bank. The farmer congratulated himself for being smart enough to hire such a sincere man who took such good care of his workers. The farmer's opinion of the contractor changed considerably when during the following week, the bad checks began pouring into the bank. Naturally the con-contractor had disappeared into the wild blue yonder happily counting thousands of dollars he had "earned" from the farmer.

As you've just learned from the case of the trusting farmer and the crooked labor contractor, not all check artists live in the city. The only protection the rural businessman or farmer has is to guard his checkbook and his checks. Whether it's a weekly salary or a seasonal salary, pay each man individually. Let no man collect for his buddy or even for his wife and children. Let the person who earned the money collect it and you'll protect yourself and your bank balance.

You shouldn't leave mail containing checks in a R. F. D. mailbox for the postman to pick up. Either hand them to the postman personally or wait until you go into town and mail them at the post office. The tenth of every month is a lucrative day for the thief who specializes in stealing checks on the rural route. The average farmer pays his bills on the tenth of the month by check and mails them by leaving the envelopes in his R. F. D. mailbox for the postman to pick up. The thief is aware of this custom and merely arrives before the mailman is due and helps himself to the mail. Frequently he'll even leave the change due the farmer, if the farmer has left money for the stamps. As a result the farmer will be completely unaware his checks have fallen into the wrong hands until he starts receiving complaints from the people to whom he owes money or until he receives his bank statement and discovers his bank account has been depleted.

Here's one thought that may save you some costly experiences. As you receive checks from customers, whether it's a small check for eggs or milk or a larger one for a load of hay you've just delivered, lock the checks in the glove compartment of your car or truck. At least it's safer than in your pocket or on the driver's seat. When you carry your checkbook with you, keep it locked in the glove compartment, too. From time to time make it a policy to count the remaining pages of checks in your blank checkbook to make sure that none have been removed.

STOP PAYMENT ORDER

Is A BANK liable for a Stop Payment Order?
Take a look at the signature card you signed at your bank
and decide for yourself.

How many times have you been pressured into giving a
salesman a check for an item you didn't really want or believe in? There is a solution though the bank will discourage
using it for this means. All you have to do is fill out and sign a
Stop Payment Order and present it in person to the bank and
the check you filled out against your will won't be honored.
Any depositor legally has the right to stop payment on checks
which he has previously drawn. Women are beginning to
know the Stop Payment Order and are using it more and
more. It might save you some money if you'd introduce your
wife to this legal means of changing her mind.

In my travels around the country and in doing research
for my book I have asked many a bank manager who is liable
for a Stop Payment Order if the check has been paid after I
have signed the card. Would you believe that thirty-five percent have told me that the bank would be liable. Now see the
card that they ask you to sign at the top of page 93 , then
decide for yourself. Some banks have revised their cards, yet
by the same token, should it come to a showdown, you can
rest assured that there will be some bickering.

If a stop payment is as effective as bankers tell me it is, why do they make you post a bond for twice the amount of a cashier's check that may be lost? Their stop payment should be as effective for them as it is for you. Draw your own conclusions.

In order to make a bank liable, a Stop Payment Order must be presented *in writing* and must be in the hands of the bank on which the stopped check is drawn *before* the check is presented for payment. Figure 18 shows an acceptable form for issuing a Stop Payment Order. A *telegram* containing the same information is legally enforceable; an *oral* or *telephoned* Stop Payment Order is not enforceable.

The first time you call the bank and insist upon giving a Stop Payment Order over the phone and you're informed you must come into the bank and sign the order personally. Knowing human nature, you'll become indignant. But the bank has a very good reason for insisting upon a signed order.

An example of what could happen is the case of two construction companies bidding against one another, the Hoffman Construction Co. and the Dunne Builders.

The Dunne Builders win the contract and give a check covering a ten percent deposit for proof of performance.

The Hoffman Construction Co. is aware of the check and the slick owner telephones his competitor's bank and requests a Stop Payment Order on the check covering the ten percent deposit.

It would not be difficult to obtain all the information needed. When the check reaches the bank and payment is stopped, it could cause the Dunne Builders a great deal of embarrassment and could lose them the contract. If it did lose the contract, the Dunne Builders could sue the bank for its losses and would win the case since the bank would be liable.

This is why it makes sense when the bank insists that you

sign the Stop Payment Order personally.

Your bank realizes its obligation in carrying out your Stop Payment Orders. It maintains careful records on all Stop Payment Orders and usually the paying tellers and check desk clerks keep alphabetical lists, according to the names of the drawers who have issued the orders, continually before them for easy reference. This order must be renewed periodically to continue its effectiveness.

A businessman who did not fully understand the bank's position in handling Stop Payment Orders telephoned his bank and requested the assistant manager to stop a check he had issued. He became quite annoyed when informed he must come into the bank and fill out the Stop Payment Order personally and sign it. He arrived later in the day quite upset about the entire situation and angrily filled out the Stop Payment Order and signed it.

In his haste and anger, he reversed the figures covering the amount and number of the check and did not notice his error. Copies of his signed Stop Payment Order were issued to the proper departments but the bank honored the check he wanted stopped since the information he had given them was incorrect. It turned out that he had written five other checks payable to the same company and they arrived at the bank with the one check the businessman wanted stopped. The bank could not run the risk of stopping payment on the wrong check and exposing itself to a lawsuit.

So *be sure* you give the bank complete and accurate information when you issue a Stop Payment Order.

If the bank does happen to pay a check that you have issued a Stop Payment Order to cover and it is the bank's error, it can be held liable only for your *actual loss,* not necessarily the total amount of the check. For example, if the check covered an insurance premium, and, as a result of the bank's payment of the check, you were actually insured and covered by the policy for a period of time, that actual

Maker	Payable to	Amount

ID 19A

To ....

STOP PAYMENT RECORD AND REQUEST

You are requested not to pay check No.........................for

$................ dated................payable to...............................

Drawn By...

Reason: ....

These directions are given with the understanding and the express condition that you will endeavor to prevent oversight and accidental payment, but you shall not be in any way liable for your act should said check be paid by you in the regular course of business. You are hereby instructed to charge my our account with customary stop payment fee.

Time......................................

Signed .... Date........................

Maker	Payable to	Amount

FROM: _____   **Date and Time Received**

               ACCOUNT NAME

TO: First Western Bank   A.M._____

and Trust Company _____Office   P. M._____

Please stop payment on check No. _____for $ _____

dated _____, 19___, payable to _____

Signed as follows:_____

The undersigned agrees (a) to notify Bank to cancel this order if and when the reason for stop payment ceases to exist; (b) that closing of the account upon which this check is drawn or its transfer to another office by the undersigned shall automatically cancel this order; and (c) that this order expires at the time as outlined in Section 994 of the State of California Financial Code.

Reason for Stop_____

Signature of Depositor_____

Address _____ Phone No._____

Stop-Payment accepted by:_____

P-150 12-62   OFFICER OR SENIOR STAFF MEMBER   (Over)

FIGURE 18
Two standard forms for Stop Payment orders. Who would you say is liable?

time could be deducted from the bank's obligation.

Unless collusion can be proved, you cannot stop payment on a check that has a second endorsement. If the person you make the check payable to had the feeling you might issue a Stop Payment Order, he may cash the check with another merchant; accepting merchandise and cash. If the merchant honorably paid out his money and merchandise, he must be repaid and the Stop Payment Order would not be effective. Only if you could prove the merchant and the payee were in league to negate the Stop Payment Order, could you legally prosecute them.

Banks have found the principal reasons businessmen issue Stop Payment Orders are to cancel a purchase order over inferior merchandise, to prevent the cashing of lost or stolen checks, and, thirdly, to prevent the payment of an original check when a duplicate of the original has already been paid.

One word of caution: Whenever you do make out a duplicate check for any reason whatsoever, before you mail it or hand it out, make sure the Stop Payment Order covering the original check is in the hands of the bank.

Whenever a payee informs you a large check has been lost or stolen, you have the right to ask the payee to post a bond covering the exact amount before you issue a duplicate check and a Stop Payment Order. Then you are fully protected in case the original check should turn up and be charged to your account. The bonding company would reimburse you.

If a stop payment is as effective as bankers tell me it is, why do they make you post a bond for twice the amount of a cashier's check that may be lost? Their stop payment should be as effective for them as it is for you. Draw your own conclusions.

CASHIER'S AND CERTIFIED CHECKS

IF YOU WANT a guarantee that a check is good, get a cashier's check or a certified check. A cashier's check is drawn on a bank. A certified check is written on your own or your firm's check. The amount to be paid out, as shown on the check, is deducted from your bank balance and the clerk stamps your check certified in three places. You will be given a receipt which you should save. Unlike your cancelled checks, a certified check does not end up in your bank statement but is retained by the bank.

You may think a cashier's or certified check is as good as the maker that guarantees it. That's not true. If all the people who handle the check are honest, then the check is good. If anyone handling that check is dishonest, then it may or may not be good.

In the past few years, I have destroyed cashier's and certified checks totalling several million dollars. I do not recall paying more than $5.00 for any 1 check. It is a known fact that there is a fast turnover in all types of banking personnel, as many business men have brought this to my attention, but I do think that the operations officer should be thoroughly trained in the correct methods of issuing such checks.

I presented a hand written check to a teller once, and asked that it be certified. The amount of the check was $5.00. When she asked me what a certified check was, I suggested that she see the operations officer. It seemed to me from where I was standing, that he knew what he was doing, until she returned and handed me the check certified, but not put through their check protector. That night, the service club I spoke to, received a gift in the form of a certified check for 1 million dollars.

As a businessman, *be cautious.* Cashier's and certified checks have an impressive, business-like appearance but use as much caution as you would in cashing a regular check. Always call the bank on which the check is drawn if you do not know for whom you are cashing it and find out whether such a check was issued.

The credit manager of a building supply firm regretted not using this service when a new contractor came into his store to purchase some expensive equipment. The contractor informed the credit manager that he wanted to pay cash until his credit was established. He filled out a check and mentioned he was going to the bank to have it certified.

The credit manager assured him the merchandise he had ordered would be packed and ready to load in his truck when the contractor returned from the bank. Within an hour the contractor was back with a certified check in the amount of $3,550.00. This was the exact price of the purchase.

The contractor left with his load of merchandise valued at $3,550.00; the credit manager later discovered he was holding a certified check valued at only $50.00.

This problem ended in the law courts. Whom would you blame?

Many people in their travels, rather than carry large amounts of cash, will buy a cashier's check which we all know to be safer. I recall a gentleman from New York who acted very irate when the manager of a Los Angeles bank refused cashing a check that had been issued from a New York bank. The customer told the manager the only reason he bought the check in the first place, was that it was supposed to be as good as cash. The manager told him it was, only when it was cleared offering to give him $50.00 in advance which the man accepted.

With regards to Money Orders, the one big fault I find with them, is that the equipment used, is not cared for in a proper manner. I have seen many money orders raised due to faulty machines. On page 104 you will see the result of what could have been an expensive lesson and a good profit to even a rank amateur check artist. These people were notified and did correct the trouble.

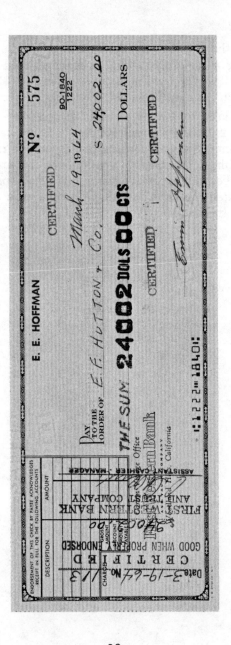

FIGURE 19

After: Errors in certified checks could be expensive.

FIGURE 20

Before: Bank teller should have recognized four errors.

99

FIGURE 21

After: Bigger banks are just as vulnerable.

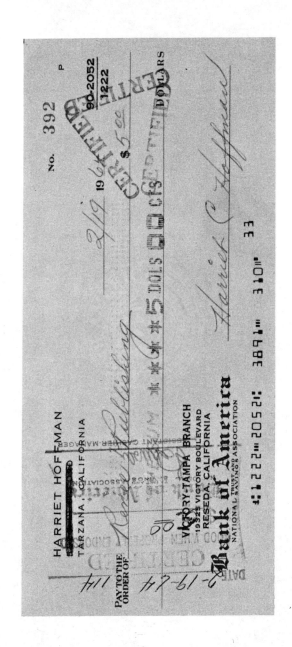

FIGURE 22

Before: Chemicals come into play at the $ sign.

102

FIGURE 23

After: Removal of stub equals net profit of $140.00.

Figure 24

Before: Carelessness is no excuse.

103

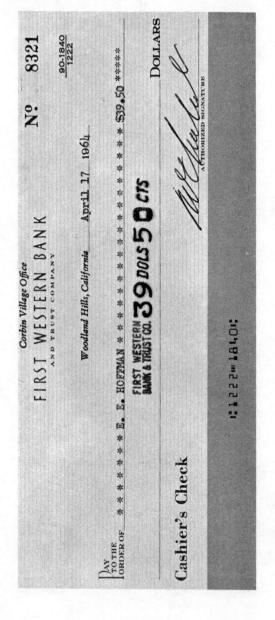

FIGURE 25

A well executed cashiers check in all respects.

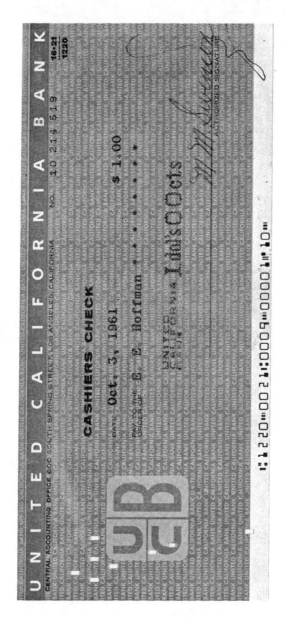

FIGURE 26

Protector plate not balanced, to much space at $ sign.

FIGURE 27

Bank should use their own protector even if maker uses one.

106

CHECK PROTECTORS

IF YOU'RE A businessman, you've certainly been visited by a check protector salesman and listened to him extoll the virtues of his particular machine. If the salesman was selling a good check protector, he pointed out how it shreds or cuts the name of the firm and the amount payable into the check and forces indelible ink into the fibre of the paper. The salesman wound up his pitch by explaining that a check protector is an inexpensive means of guarding against losing money through altered checks.

You probably were impressed with its features and agreed with the salesman that every business should own a check protector. But you probably decided to "think it over" or thought you'd "shop around for a bargain."

If you write any business checks, one altered check could cost you more than a good check protector and the bargain you're looking for may not really protect your checks.

The *one* machine that could be more valuable than an adding machine in an office today is a *good* check protector. No business is too small to use some sort of protective device on its checks.

As early at 1870 a form of check protector was manufactured. It consisted of individual punches which perforated figure holes in the paper, similar to the cancelling machines used by banks to show the date a check is paid. The amount of protection this early protector gave is doubtful. Twenty-nine years later a check protector appeared that forced ink into the paper under pressure, making it part of the fiber of the document. This was done by turning dials and spinning a handle that would advance each number of the amount. This was not only time consuming, but mistakes sometimes occurred.

The improvements and new features you'll find in a modern check protector include smooth, fast operational efficiency, quite unlike the early machines. Most of today's machines use paste ink, while some use ribbons. Many manufacturers provide a system for locking the machine when not in use so only authorized personnel control it. One manufacturer has both a system for locking the machine and an alarm system which automatically sets off a signal when the machine is picked up. Some check protector companies will issue an insurance policy which guarantees reimbursement for forged or altered checks. This policy is usually included in the purchase price of the check protector.

If you're a businessman who should be in the market for a modern check protector, don't approach the purchase as you would a new automobile. A new model doesn't come out every year. There are at least five companies manufacturing check protectors. *Not all are as safe as the manufacturer would have you believe.* All check protectors have the same objective . . . to penetrate the fibers of the paper. Prices vary according to the size and style of machine that is installed.

There is a so-called check protector on the market, sometimes given away as a free premium, and in other cases it sells for about $3.50. It is a plier-type instrument with rollers that will perforate the written or typed payee's name and the amount payable. No ink is used. The salesman neglects to inform the customer that these perforations can be straightened out by running a fingernail over the back of the check, closing up the perforations. *Know* the machine you buy and make sure it *really will* protect your firm.

The check protector that cuts a firm name or registered number right next to the first figure of the check is the safest type of check protector. If the name of your firm is cut into the check, *make sure* the plate or die moves over *to meet* the first figure.

A good example is shown in Fig. 8, p. 55. There is no way to insert another figure without removing the perforated firm name.

Guard against the malfunctioning machine in which the bar that would have your firm name, or the words "THE SUM" FAIL TO MOVE OVER TO THE FIRST FIGURE, for the amount of the check. This is illustrated in FIG. 42 . Although the check was sold to me for $1.00, after the first glance, I told the market manager he should have his machine fixed. He politely told me that no one could change the amount and he was not concerned. His whole attitude changed when I returned the $90.00 after cashing same at his store. See Figure 41.

If a check protector uses a series of markings, such as stars, triangles or a dollar sign, next to the first figure of the check, you will find this type of machine is usually unsafe. Examples of checks protected by these machines are shown in Figures 38, and 40. If the markings are removed, the thief could easily add another figure raising the check's value without returning to the office to use the firm's check protector. See Figures 37, and 39.

If the check protector you are now using is fifteen or twenty years old, it is time to retire it. It may be cutting or printing good, but there is more to it than appears on the surface. Check artists are keeping up with the times, and in most cases can beat these machines. Don't compare the age of a check

109

protector with other office equipment. As long as your adding machine, regardless of age, ads correct, you are safe. Characters on a new typewriter are the same as they were thirty years ago, yet what benefit would any one get by trying to change "A" to a "C" on a letter? The improvements in the current models of good check protectors are aimed at giving you the most effective protection.

Still further protection can be had if you will have the bank print the following on your checks, NOT VALID FOR MORE THAN $200.00. This is especially valuable on payroll checks. In some cases, it may be necessary to vary the amounts according to the type of business you are engaged in. This is just an added precaution. Should anyone devise a means of obliterating or erasing the imprint, the bank could not be held liable. Printers ink is very hard to erase.

For firms who will have a secretary or bookkeeper write the checks and then bring them in for signing, be sure that the check protector has already been used. Do not sign the check as shown in Fig. 44. The owner of a large printing firm had this sad experience to the tune of $9,000.00. The first time his bookkeeper asked him to sign some checks, he asked why she did not protect them? Her answer was that the ink on the machine was to wet, and he might smear them, while in the process of signing. It was several months later, when they had an audit, they found out that after he had signed all the checks, she ran them through the machine for a larger amount making a slight change in the figure part. See Fig. 43.

If you are using a good check protector, are you availing yourself of the protection it should give you? When did you last ink or change the ribbon on your machine? I have seen many checks put through check protectors where the ink was so light, they would have been better off to type or write the entire check in long hand. The only way you could tell what the amount of the check, was written for, was to look at the figure near the $ sign.

Note the lightness of the check in Fig. 34. Using the same same type machine which was properly inked, the figure "8" was stamped over the existing "3". Fig. 33. This would have not been possible, if the first imprint had enough ink. The figure 3 could not have been covered without showing through.

By checking your equipment against the illustrations in the next 18 pages, you can determine for yourself whether your equipment is giving you the protection you paid for. You may be the 1 person in 8 who keeps their check protector in good order. The professional check artist is keeping his eyes on the other 7.

If you're financially unable to purchase any type of check protector, there is one means of protecting your checks at no cost to you.

After the check has been completely filled out and signed, *apply clear plastic tape* over the payee's name and the numbered amount of the check. If anyone should try to remove the tape to alter the check the aniline dye coating on the "safety paper" would be removed and the check could not be cashed. Figure 45 shows an example.

On some checks that have a very hard coating, it may be necessary after applying the tape to pull the corner up fast, then when the peeling has started, press back into place and it will remain indefinitely.

Some banks object to this procedure, as it reduces the efficiency of their perforating equipment; it should only be used in extreme cases where a reliable check protector is not available.

If your check protector should need any service or repairs, it is best that you contact the salesman or firm that originally sold it to you. If your machine is under two years old, in most cases it would be covered by the original guarantee and there would be no charge.

Before you let anyone walk out the door with your check machine for service make sure you know the firm he represents. I know of one firm that employs solicitors to call on

111

firms just to pick up check protectors for repairs. They will leave a loaner to use until they can determine the cost of the cleaning or adjusting and after a week, will call and tell the owner there was more wrong with the machine than was anticipated. In some cases, all the machine needed was an ink assembly or just ink, but they found out, to get the machine back in working order, it cost them almost half of what they paid for it originally.

All manufacturers of check protectors, due to the nature of their business, will issue I.D. cards to all their salesmen. Ask for this card before you let anyone check your machine.

FIGURE 28

Latest type raise proof figures if machine properly maintained.

113

FIGURE 29
After alteration.

114

FIGURE 30
Before alteration.

FIGURE 31

After alteration.

116

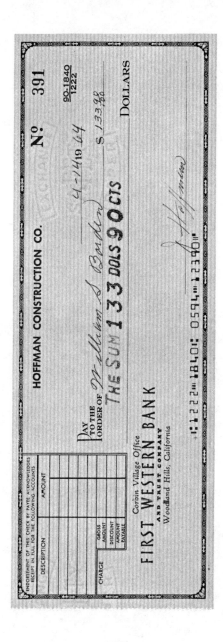

FIGURE 32

Before alteration.

117

FIGURE 33

After: Five hundred dollars a tube is expensive.

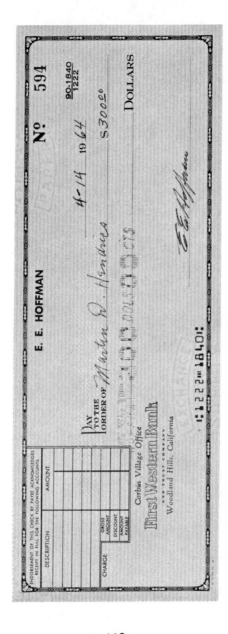

FIGURE 34

Before: From the looks of this check, ink is expensive.

119

FIGURE 35

After alteration.

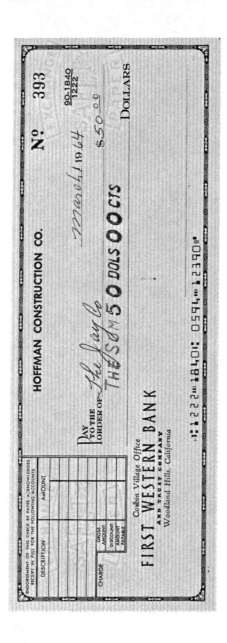

Figure 36

Before alteration.

121

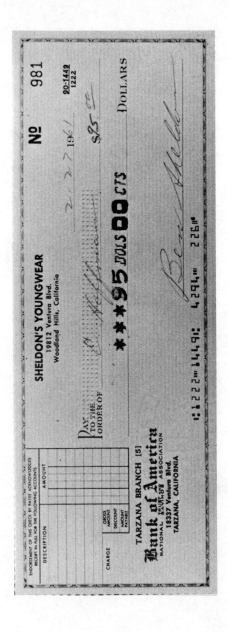

FIGURE 37

After alteration.

123

FIGURE 39
After alteration.

124

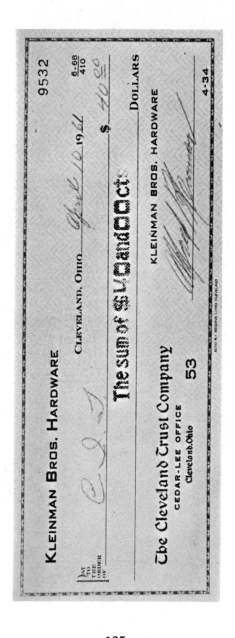

FIGURE 40
Before alteration.

125

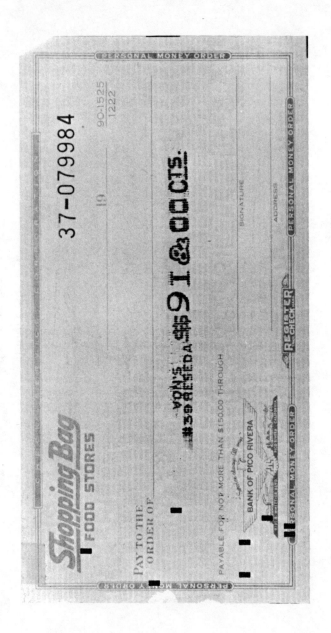

F<small>IGURE</small> 41

After: Although a larger figure "9" was used to alter check, a clerk at the market was ready to cash the check for $91.00.

Figure 42

Before: Check-writing machine was not in proper working order. Note space between $ and amount.

FIGURE 43

After: Bank not responsible.

FIGURE 44

Before: Do not sign checks until completely filled in.

129

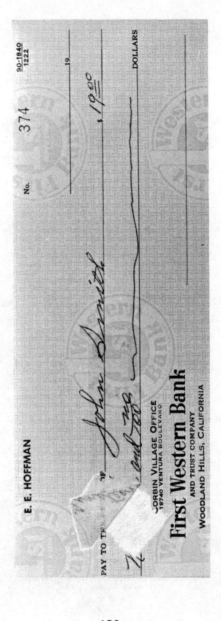

FIGURE 45

Readily available method of check protection. (See Page 111).

CHECK SIGNERS

If you are considering the installation of a check signing machine, there are several things you should take into consideration. First, the person who will be entrusted to use it should be under bond unless he is the owner. Second, do you have a safe place to keep the unit or the signature bar? Third, and most important, do you have a place to store the blank checks? This I think is the most important. Your bank will then have you sign a "facsimile signature" statement shown in Fig.46 for its files. This is self explanatory.

For your protection most signers are equipped with keys. Some make the unit so the signature bar can be removed and tucked in a vault or the person responsible for its use can carry it on his person. All machines are made with a counter that cannot be reset by any employee. If the counter reads 3509 at the beginning of the day and you know that 150 checks were written on that day, the counter should read 3659. Should it read 3669, better have someone account for the 10 checks that are floating around signed.

With all the precautions that the manufacturers have taken, the businessman could still have a problem. Many businesses that use this type of equipment are of course larger firms. They usually order checks in large quantities which are packed from 500 to 1000 per carton. I have seen these cartons marked as to contents stored wherever it was most handy for the operator to get to. I was called into a large firm one day as a consultant for a check problem, and after the problem was resolved, the owner wanted to show me his new signer, protector, and dater which he told me was the best equipment on the market. I told him for what he paid for it, it had to be the best. He showed me four different keys that were required to operate it, explaining that he has full control. As we were walking towards the exit together, I noticed a box of checks lying on one of the desks in the office. I did make a remark that they should have been put away. He informed me again that the checks are not valid as they were not signed. It was then, he got the shock of his life. I asked if I might have one of the checks that were signed with the machine. He gave me a cancelled check that was one month old. I removed one check from the box that was on the desk, and with the aid of my past experiences, I transferred the signature from the cancelled check to the new check without going near his $3500.00 machine. He could not tell that the signer was NOT used. Now he keeps all checks locked up.

I_____ authorize, request, and direct Security First National Bank as a designated depositary of this account to honor all checks, drafts or other orders for the payment of money drawn in this account number _620_ (including those drawn to the individual order of any person or persons whose names appear thereon as signer or signers thereof) when bearing or pur porting to bear the facsimile signature of the following:

_____
John Doe

and said bank (including its correspondent banks) shall be entitled to honor and to charge this account for all such checks, drafts or other orders for the payment of money, regardless of by whom or by what means the actual or purported facsimile signature thereon may have been affixed thereto, if such facsimile signature resembles the facsimile specimens from time to time filed with said Bank.

FURTHER: That all previous authorizations for the signing and honoring of checks, drafts or other orders for the payment of money drawn on said Bank by us are hereby continued in full force and effect as amplified hereby.

FIGURE 46

Standard form to be signed prior to installing signer.

133

FIGURE 47

Which one of the two is a counterfeit?

134

FIGURE 48

Ask if your signer is bonded against the counterfeiter.

135

Your bank can hold you responsible for any loopholes the check artist finds in your checks. There are thousands of pen changes that can be made by "doctoring" the amount written on the "Dollar" line. People that have been writing checks for many years, frequently state, "When I write a check, I am sure no one can raise it, because I always start to the far left hand side of the line". It is true that many people leave some space to where another word could be added, but this is done mostly by women.

I certainly do not want to discredit our educators, but in all the classes that I have attended in business administration, as a guest, was there sufficient information given to the students on the proper procedures for the safety measures to be used in writing or typing checks. Ninety per cent of the graduates did not know the proper way to safeguard their personal checks, let alone the checks they would be required to write for their employers.

If you will write the figure 1 eight times, you will see how easy it is to change them to read 2, 4, 5, 6, 7, 8, 9 or 0. It is true, that the figures on a check have to correspond with the amount on the dollar line, before the bank will honor it. This is no problem to the professional check artist. As you look at pages 140 to 159, you will see that many amounts written in long hand can be altered as easily as the figures. *Never write the amount on the dollar line, this should be printed.* Figure 62 shows a check in the amount of Sixteen dollars. Figure 63 is the same check now payable for Sixty-Six. If the check were

SIXTH-GRADE BOY ARRESTED FOR STEALING CHECKS

A sixth-grader today had been arrested for taking three checks out of a mailbox, but North Hollywood juvenile officers expect to rebook the boy soon on a forgery charge.

It seems the 10-year-old erased the payee's name on one check, inserted his own and cashed it at a local butcher shop. How did he make the check look normal? He used a colored pencil to fix the discolored portions, he told officers.

Sgt. L. W. Gandre of the Juvenile Bureau said the youth was released to his mother pending a Juvenile Court hearing.

The boy said he hadn't altered the other two checks and he would return them to police.

hand printed, this would have been impossible. Although the word four is spell with a (u), changing it to forty was easily accomplished because of our way of spelling. See Figures 52 and 53. It is amazing how many people will tell me when I raise their check for four to forty, that I have misspelled the word forty, as I did not spell it with a (u). Checks that are the easiest to change are the amounts of six, seven, eight or nine. It is also possible to make a double change as shown in Figure 54.

Many people seem to be under the impression that when they send a check to a reputable firm, that no one can cash the check except the firm to whom the check to made payable. This holds true except when the check has not been properly filled out. I have been able to cash checks made payable to reputable firms only because the words Company, Brothers, Incorporated or the initials such as G.M.A.C. were abbreviated. When I ask a bookkeeper why he did not spell out the entire word, the answer is, "It takes too much time". Look at some of the checks that are illustrated, and you will see that many firm name checks can be altered to read another name. Bear in mind that banks are not obligated to know the names of all the people you do business with nor can you except them to be mind readers.

If you use a bookkeeping machine for making out checks, such as shown in Figure 64, you're asking for trouble. Newer machines will insert asterisks (*) in front of the figure so as to make it more difficult to add to the amount.

With penmanship being what it is today, there is no doubt in my mind that typing the body of a check is by far the neatest and most legible. There again, we have one major loophole that could cost you your bank balance. See Figure 60 and note the space between the $ sign and the first figure. Figure 61 will show how easy it was to insert another figure. The protector made the rest easy. YOU NEVER KNOW WHO IS GOING TO HANDLE YOUR CHECKS, SO MAKE THEM OUT WITH CARE. DON'T TEMPT PEOPLE.

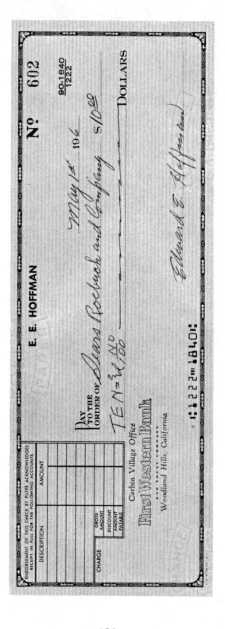

FIGURE 49

Safest method for handwritten checks.

FIGURE 50

Before alteration: Abbreviations are not safe on checks.

140

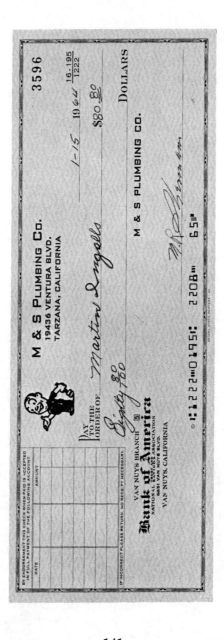

FIGURE 51
After alteration.

FIGURE 52

After alteration.

FIGURE 53

Before alteration.

143

Figure 54

After alteration: Many double changes are possible.

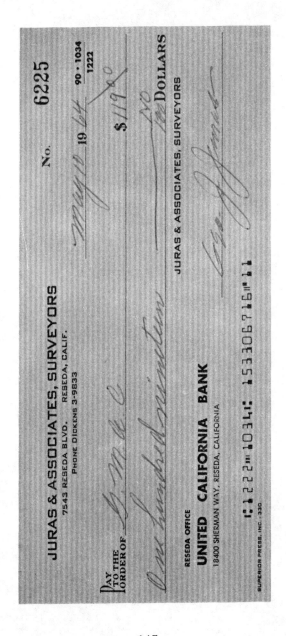

FIGURE 55
Before alteration.

FIGURE 56

Before: Too much space on left side of dollar line.

146

FIGURE 57

After: Does the word "hundred" have to be written?

FIGURE 58

Before: Close up all spaces on dollar line.

148

FIGURE 59

After: Using the wide open spaces to a good advantage.

149

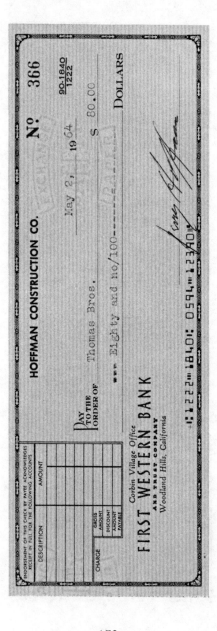

FIGURE 60
Before: Don't leave any spaces between $ sign and first figure.

FIGURE 61

After: Can you read typing under check machine imprint?

151

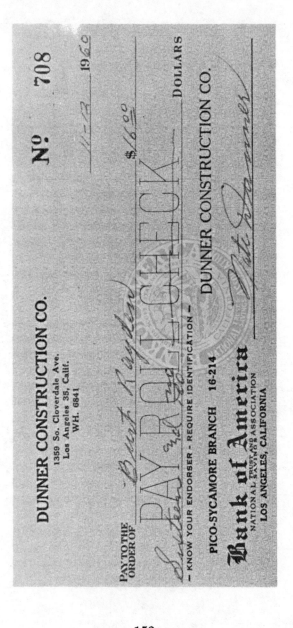

FIGURE 62

After: Hand printing amount would have prevented this.

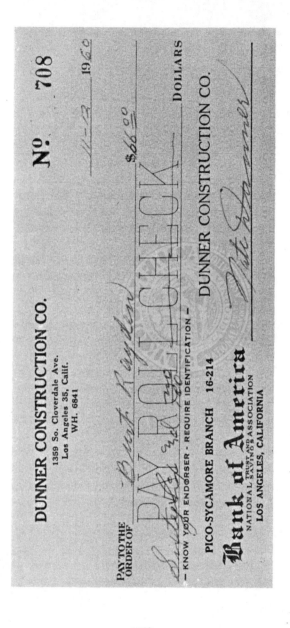

FIGURE 63

Before: Don't write, but print amount on dollar line.

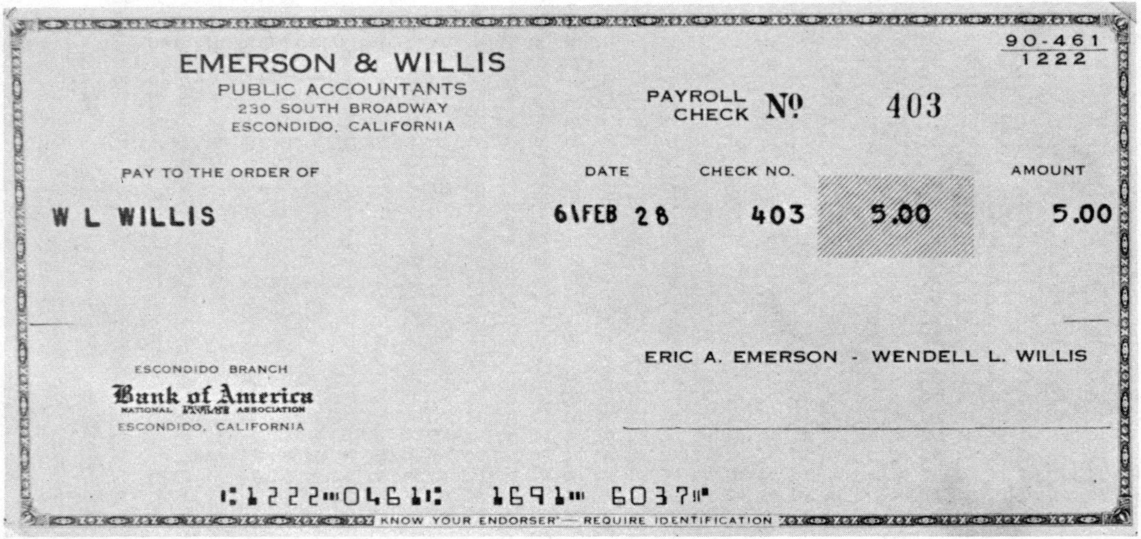
90-461
1222

EMERSON & WILLIS
PUBLIC ACCOUNTANTS
230 SOUTH BROADWAY
ESCONDIDO, CALIFORNIA

PAYROLL CHECK Nº 403

PAY TO THE ORDER OF	DATE	CHECK NO.		AMOUNT
W L WILLIS	61FEB 28	403	5.00	5.00

ESCONDIDO BRANCH
Bank of America
NATIONAL TRUST AND SAVINGS ASSOCIATION
ESCONDIDO, CALIFORNIA

ERIC A. EMERSON - WENDELL L. WILLIS

⑆1222⑉0461⑆ 1691⑉ 6037⑈

KNOW YOUR ENDORSER — REQUIRE IDENTIFICATION

FIGURE 64
Before: Asterisks should precede first figure to force an erasure.

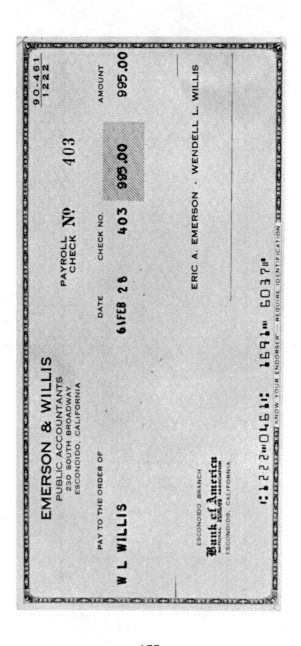

FIGURE 65

After: Don't expect your bank to be a mind reader.

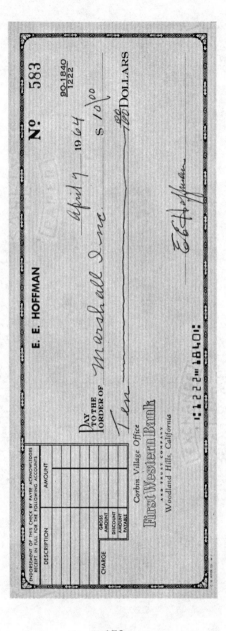

FIGURE 66
Before: Note payee.

FIGURE 67
After: Note payee.

157

FIGURE 68

After: Loss charged to maker.

FIGURE 69

Before: Too much space at $ sign.

159

COMMON SAFETY RULES TO PRACTICE

Don't write checks with lead or dry indelible pencil.

Don't abbreviate words such as Company, Corporation, Incorporated or payee names such as G.M.A.C. or C.I.T.

Don't leave any spaces between the dollar sign and the first figure especially if typing a check.

Don't write, but print the amount on the dollar line, then four can't be changed to forty as shown in Figs. 52 and 53.

Don't sign checks in the book with a ballpoint pen, if you have a heavy hand. The imprint goes through the underneath check. Remove from book before signing.

Don't have your checks imprinted at the top the way your signature appears at the bottom. It should be different.

Don't expose your bank balance at a public counter while making out a check.

Don't leave your blank printed checks exposed to strangers who may be in your office or shop.

Don't leave your cancelled checks lying around where any outsider may get to them.

Don't sign a check until it has been filled in completely.

Don't let the inking mechanism of your check protector get too light.

Don't keep surplus monies in checking account, transfer it to savings account.

Follow these simple rules, forget many of your former habits you have practiced, and for a certainty you will give the check artist a bad time. Remember, one of the most valuable assets in your office is your checkbook. Cooperate with the banks and everyone will be better off. Many a businessman has found out the hard way, you can't beat a man at his own game.